VISIT THE CITY

3 Days in

# FRANKFURT

Make the most of your time!

# FRANKFURT AT A GLANCE

# Content

**Legend**

- ⌛ Duration of the tour
- ◆ Opening times/ departure times
- ▲ Transport stop
- ➤ see


3/4/17

**Editor in chief:**
Dr. Brigitte Hintzen-Bohlen

**Design:**
BKB Kommunikation
Andreas Ossig
www.bkb-kommunikation.de

**Translation:**
John Sykes

**Printed by:**
Brandt GmbH, Bonn

ISBN 978-3-940914-35-4



BKB Verlag
Auerstraße 4
50733 Köln
Telephone 0049-2221/9521460
Fax 0049-2221/5626446
www.bkb-verlag.de
mail@bkb-verlag.de

# Welcome to

... the international finance and trade fair centre on the river Main with its impressive skyline and long history, where towers of steel and glass, idyllic half-timbered buildings and fine 19th-century residences combine with traditional pubs selling apple wine, leafy parks and lively shopping streets to form a synthesis that is sometimes breathtaking. The contrasts of the traditional and the modern, history and banking, trade fairs and culture are anything but boring.

The city on the Main is 1200 years old, and as young today as it ever was. Thanks to Frankfurt's site on the river and at the intersection of important trade routes, industry, commerce and banking blossomed here

# Frankfurt ...

back in the Middle Ages. The trade fair was founded as long ago as 1150, the exchange in 1585. Frankfurt was a Free Imperial City, where kings and emperors were crowned and later German democracy began. The people of Frankfurt have always played a leading role and shown active commitment to their city – as patrons, for example of the Städel Museum or the university, or in citizens' initiatives such as those to preserve the old opera house or the Westend.

In all periods, the people of Frankfurt have given a high priority to art and culture. It was the home of the greatest poet of the German language, Goethe. The world's oldest jazz festival was founded here, and techno music was born in the city. It has a unique "museum mile" and the world's largest book fair. To this day the city can justly be proud of its extensive and varied cultural life, which combines the established with the experimental. Wherever you look, great importance is attached to the quality of life. The nightlife of Frankfurt, whether it takes place in a traditional pub serving Ebbelwoi (apple wine) or in a modern club, is as exciting as the skyline with its imperial cathedral and Commerzbank Tower. On all sides there is something new and thrilling to be discovered. Enjoy yourself!

# About Frankfurt

● There is more than one FRANKFURT! No fewer than 26 cities all over the world have the same name as the one on the river Main. In addition to Frankfurt an der Oder on the Polish border, in Germany there is also a Frankfurt in Bavaria and one in Sachsen-Anhalt. In the USA, Canada, Ireland, South Africa and Australia, the German spelling has become Frankfort or Frankford.

● Although Frankfurt's inhabitants, drawn from 180 countries, number only about 720,000, on every working day it becomes a CITY OF A MILLION. Some 300,000 commuters come in daily for their work.

● As the SEAT OF THE EUROPEAN CENTRAL BANK, Frankfurt is Euro Town. Decisions on monetary policy are taken here for almost 340 million people.

● Since the completion of the DomRömer Quarter, the citizens of Frankfurt have again been able to walk the old CORONATION WAY from the Römer to the imperial cathedral, as many rulers of the Holy Roman Empire once did.

● Frankfurt produces its own HONEY: from twelve hives on the roof of Museum für Moderne Kunst, every year approximately 650,000 bees buzz off to gather pollen for Frankfurt museum honey.

● In Frankfurt you can ride in a PATERNOSTER: in Fleming's Deluxe Hotel Frankfurt-City, a historic elevator of this kind takes guests to the 7th floor, where there is a fine view across the city from the roof terrace.

● Frankfurt has 13 of the 15 TALLEST BUILDINGS in Germany. The highest skyscraper at present is the Commerzbank Tower at 259 metres.

● One of the tallest WOODEN VIEWING TOWERS in Germany also stands in Frankfurt: in the Waldspielpark

you can look out over the green belt, the skyline and in clear conditions the whole Rhine-Main region from the 43-metre Goetheturm.

● In NICE, a park on the banks of the Main, you will feel as if you are in a garden on the French Riviera. Many Mediterranean plants grow here thanks to the south-facing location sheltered from the wind.

● SAFETY MATCHES come from Frankfurt, where the chemist Rudolph Christian Boettger (1806-1881) invented matches with red phosphor in 1848.

● Alongside the Weissenhofsiedlung in Stuttgart and the Bauhaus in Dessau, NEW FRANKFURT (Neues Frankfurt) is one of the most important examples of early Modernist architecture in Germany. As a remedy for the shortage of affordable housing during the Weimar Republic, the urban planner, head of housing and architect Ernst May (1886–1970) initiated a project that created around 15,000 affordable homes.

● The world's FIRST FITTED KITCHEN was invented by the Viennese architect Margarete Schütte-Lihotzky (1897-2000) for the New Frankfurt housing project: the so-called Frankfurt kitchen was a standard fitting, designed to optimise work processes.

# 3 Days in

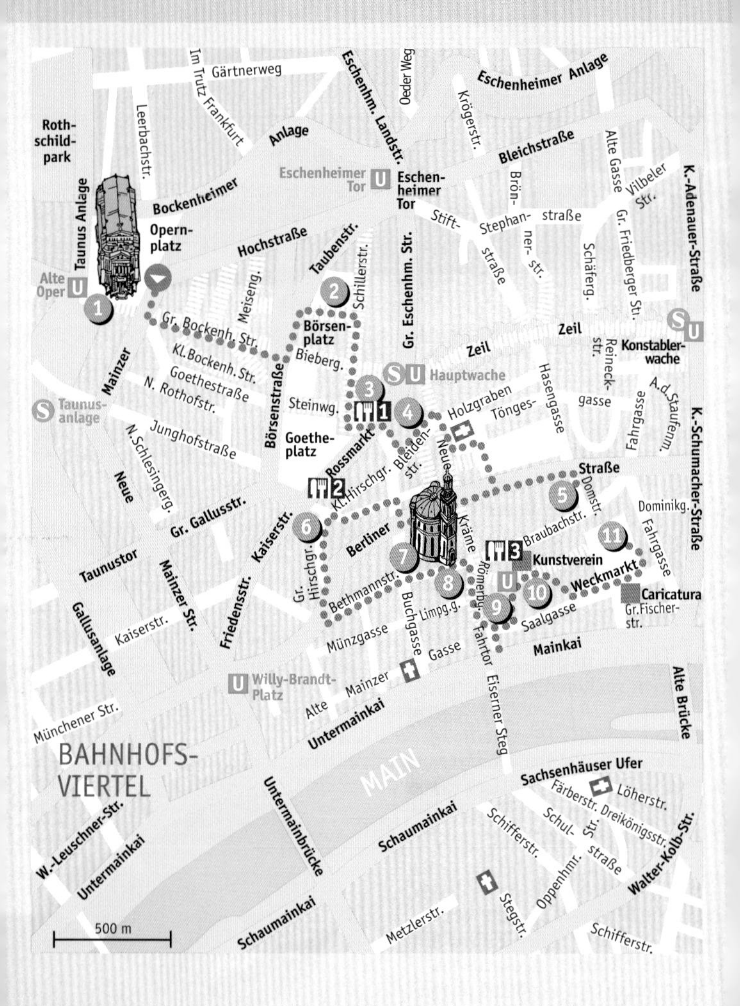


1 Alte Oper
2 Börse
3 Hauptwache
4 Katharinenkirche
5 Museum für Moderne Kunst
6 Goethe-Museum/ Goethe-Haus
7 Paulskirche
8 Römer
9 Alte Nikolaikirche
10 Schirn Kunsthalle
11 Dom St. Bartholomäus

1 Café Hauptwache
2 Café Walden
3 Cafébar im Kunstverein

# A City Stroll

## A CITY STROLL – CITIZENS, BANKERS AND DEMOCRATS

*This walk around the city centre reveals what citizens' efforts can achieve, what the bull and bear stand for and how Frankfurt's most famous son lived.*

**Alte Oper**
*Opernplatz 1*
*Tours:*
*Tel. 0173/9657144*
*www.alteoper.de*

The tour starts on Opernplatz at the Alte Oper, a monumental late classical building in High Renaissance style that is seen as Germany's most beautiful concert hall and was dedicated by the citizens of Frankfurt to "Truth, Beauty, Virtue". Pegasus, the winged horse on which all poets ride, stands in symbolic majesty on the roof, and a quadriga of panthers that once adorned the city theatre crowns the gable.

Whereas the exterior has been almost completely restored to its original appearance, visitors get a surprise after entering: within the historic outer walls the reconstruction created an entirely new interior that meets the technical requirements of a concert hall and modern congress centre. Only the foyer and vestibule recall the original interior fittings of the opera house as it was designed by the architect, Richard Lucae.

**"The finest ruin in Germany"**
The Frankfurt opera house shows twice over what civic spirit can achieve. The opera, which opened on 20 October 1880 in the presence of Emperor Wilhelm I with a performance of Mozart's *Don Giovanni*, was built thanks to the donations of wealthy citizens. It was so magnificent that the emperor enviously commented he could not afford such an opera house in Berlin. When it burned out in the Second World War, one of the earliest citizens' initiatives in the Federal Republic pushed through reconstruction against the will of the city authorities – the economics minister of Hesse and later mayor, Rudi Arndt, actually wanted to demolish it in 1965 "with a bit of dynamite". And almost 40 years after the end of the war, on 28 August 1981, the opera house was ceremoniously opened once again.

### Fressgass

Continue the walk along Grosse Bockenheimer Strasse, probably Frankfurt's best-known street for a culinary stroll, which has now officially been given the name *Fressgass* ("eat street"). Here delicatessens, cafés and restaurants rub shoulders and invite passers-by to stop for a snack. The street already had its nickname around 1900 because it was the larder for the Westend, then a residential area favoured by high-class citizens, and was home to an unusually large number of butchers, bakers, delicatessens and old-established eating houses.

### Börse

*Börsenplatz 2–6*
*Visitor centre:*
*◆ by appointement only: Tel. 069/21111515*
*www.deutsche-boerse.com*

Take a short detour to the building in front of which massive sculptures of a bull and bear symbolise rising and falling share values respectively. The Frankfurt stock exchange (Börse) has its seat in this monumental domed edifice, built in neo-Renaissance style in 1874–79. If you want to find out whether the trading floor is still filled with wildly gesticulating dealers who communicate by sign language and make agreements by shouting, book a tour at the visitor centre.

In the introductory talk you get acquainted with the activity on the exchange in 45 minutes, learn the basics of floor and Xetra trading, and can take a look at traditional floor trading.

**Frankfurt and the exchange**

Thanks to its famous trade fairs, in the 16th century Frankfurt was a prosperous city which drew in merchants from all over Europe. However, as Germany was then a patchwork of little states, each with its own currency, the monetary situation was confusing. That is why trade fair merchants got together in 1585 to set unified rates of exchange. This was the origin of the Frankfurt stock exchange. More than 200 years later this primarily private association became a public institution, which took its place alongside London and Paris in the 19th century as a global exchange. And has remained so to this day!

## Hauptwache

This spacious square, where once criminals were executed or punished in the stocks, is a good place for a break. It takes its name from the single-storey Baroque building with a lovely arcade which was the main watch station of the city defence force and also contained a prison, where among others the famous brigand captain Schinderhannes was held.

*»Have a break«*

**Café Hauptwache** is a pleasant place from which to watch people coming and going in the city, with a classic Frankfurt snack or just a cup of coffee. *An der Hauptwache 15*
*◆ Mon-Sat 10am-11pm, Sun 10am-10pm*

## Katharinenkirche

*◆ Mon-Sat noon-6pm*
*www.st-katharinengemeinde.de*

The city's main Protestant church, which stands on the south side of the square, originated in two 14th-century chapels that stood next to each other. They belonged to a nunnery for noble maidens that was dedicated to St Catherine and to an almshouse built by the patrician Wicker Frosch in 1343. When Frankfurt became a Lutheran city, they were combined to form a church and replaced in 1681 by an imposing new building with a conspicuous flanking tower.

Owing to destruction in the war, nothing remains of the formerly magnificent Baroque interior of this hall church, where the Goethe family once attended services. Today the principal adornment consists of the 17 windows of stained glass, on which the artist Charles Crodel painted biblical scenes in 1953.

**Legendary beginnings**
The name Frankfurt derives from the word Frankonovurd, the "ford of the Franks" – a place where the river Main could be crossed safely. This ford is the subject of a legend, according to which Charlemagne founded the city. During his wars against the Saxons, while he was retreating and searching for a river crossing for his army, a white hart is said to have come to his aid. It crossed the Main at a shallow place, thus showing Charlemagne's soldiers a way to safety on the opposite bank – and so giving birth to Frankonovurd.

**3 TIP** The church, at which the German composer Georg Philipp Telemann (1681–1767) was master of music, is known as a centre for religious music thanks to frequent organ concerts and performances by the *Kantorei St. Katharinen*.
See *www.stk-musik.de* for the programme.

**Museum für Moderne Kunst**
*Domstrasse 10 (MMK1),*
*Domstrasse 3 (MMK3),*
▲ *Römer, Domstrasse*
◆ *Tue, Thu-Sun 10am-6pm,*
*Wed 10am-8pm*
*www.mmk-frankfurt.de*

Via *Liebfrauenberg* you will reach a museum that is known locally as the *"slice of cake"* because of its triangular shape. In 1983 Hans Hollein, a Viennese architect, produced a spectacular design for a three-storey gallery on this challenging three-sided site. In approximately 40 interior spaces he unfolded a series of transitions and connections, creating new and unexpected lines of sight.

If the fascinating architecture is not sufficient reason for a visit, the collection of art definitely is, as it is one of Europe's highlights. The basis of the holdings is the collection of Karl Ströher, a businessman from Darmstadt, which includes whole groups of works by such well-known proponents of Pop Art as Roy Lichtenstein, Claes Oldenburg and Andy Warhol, and has been systematically expanded to take in the latest statements of international contemporary art.

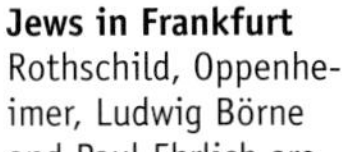

**Jews in Frankfurt**
Rothschild, Oppenheimer, Ludwig Börne and Paul Ehrlich are just a few well-known names from Frankfurt's Jewish community, which had a decisive influence on the cultural, economic and political life of the city from the mid-19th century. Foundations such as the university and the Städelscher Museums-Verein and institutions such as the Frankfurter Allgemeine Zeitung owed their existence to Jewish patrons, and the great majority of financial business was carried out by Jews. Until 1933 this community, which dates back to the 12th century, was 60,000 strong, accounting for 6.3 per cent of the total population. You can find out more about the past lives of Jews in Frankfurt in the *Museum Judengasse*.

*Kurt-Schumacher-Strasse 10*
*(city centre)*
▲ *Börneplatz*
◆ *Tue, Thu-Sun 10am-6pm,*
*Wed 10am-8pm*
*www.judengasse.de*
*www.juedisches museum.de*

**Goethe-Museum/Goethe-Haus**
*Am grossen Hirschgraben 23–25*
▲ *Willy-Brandt-Platz*
◆ *Mon-Sat 10am-6pm, Sun 10am-5.30pm*
*www.goethehaus-frankfurt.de*

From modern art we go back into the 18th century in Grosser Hirschgraben, site of the parental home of Frankfurt's greatest son: in this house, where *Götz von Berlichingen* and *The Sorrows of Young Werther* were written, Johann Wolfgang Goethe was born on 28 August 1749 "at the stroke of twelve".

The present building, a reconstruction of the house of Goethe's parents, is an attractive example of 18th-century living and the styles in vogue at that time. Note the original water pump that has been preserved in the *kitchen* on the ground floor! While other residents had to fetch their water from the public well, here the pump was connected to a well in the cellar.

In the *Kabinett* exhibition you can find out everything about the house and its inhabitants, as well as about Goethe's life in Frankfurt and his early work. It is a special experience to visit the *Dichterzimmer*, the room in which Goethe wrote his early works.

*»Have a break«* 2

If you need a break after spending time with the prince of poets, relax with coffee and cake in **Walden**.
*Kleiner Hirschgraben 7*
◆ *Mon-Sat 9am-1am, Sun 9am-6pm*

**Poetry and truth**

In his autobiography entitled *Dichtung und Wahrheit* (Poetry and Truth), Germany's greatest poet, Johann Wolfgang von Goethe (1749–1832) described his Frankfurt years: born to a wealthy family, he studied law in Leipzig at his father's wish and opened a small legal practice in 1771. However, poetry was always more important to him, and the period before he took ministerial office at court in Weimar was one of the most productive of his life. *The Sorrows of Young Werther*, inspired by his unrequited love for Charlotte Buff, quickly made him famous all over Europe. At the same time in Frankfurt he wrote *Götz von Berlichingen*, dramas such as *Clavigo* and *Stella*, and took the execution of Susanna Margaretha Brandt, who murdered her child, as the basis of the tragedy of Gretchen in *Faust*.

## Paulskirche

*Paulsplatz 11 ◆ 10am-5pm*

Bethmannstrasse leads to an oval, Neoclassical sandstone building that is the pre-eminent symbol of German democracy: St Paul's Church. On 18 May 1848 the National Assembly, the first freely elected parliament representing the whole of Germany, convened here to prepare German unification and a constitution for a united Germany. Although the establishment of a nation state was prevented by the interests of the Prussian and Austrian monarchies, important parts of the constitution were incorporated in the Basic Law of the Federal Republic of Germany. That is why John F. Kennedy described the Paulskirche as the cradle of democracy when he visited Germany in 1963. Today a gigantic mural painted by the Berlin artist Johannes Grutzke, *The Procession of People's Representatives*, can be seen in the church, which was once the city's main Protestant place of worship, and the 28-metre-high ceremonial hall is used for public events such as the award of the Peace Prize of the German Book Trade.

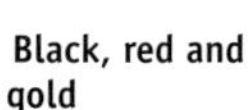

### Black, red and gold

When a seat for the National Assembly was sought after the March revolution, the Paulskirche as the largest church in the city seemed particularly suitable. As the pre-parliament met here already in late March to prepare elections for the National Assembly, the church had to be transformed quickly: banners in the national colours black, red and gold decorated the walls and windows, a curtain depicting Germania veiled the organ, and the president's desk stood in front of the altar and pulpit. Thus, on 18 May 1848, the elected representatives under their president Heinrich von Gagern were able to enter the church for their first session, to the sound of bells and firing cannon.

## RÖMER – ON THE CORONATION WAY

*To end the day, this walk goes to the city's most famous landmark, the seat of government in Frankfurt for over 600 years, and to the place were German coronations were celebrated.*

**Electing the king, crowning the emperor**
It must have been an exciting moment when the prince electors withdrew to the so-called Electoral Chapel in the south of the choir of St Bartholomew and afterwards proclaimed the newly elected king from the rood screen. The Golden Bull of 1356 laid down what had become almost the rule since Frederick Barbarossa was elected German king in 1152: the election took place in St Bartholomew's Church in Frankfurt, the coronation in the royal chapel in Aachen. However, in 1562 the Habsburgs decided to combine the two ceremonies, and up to 1806 ten Holy Roman Emperors of the German Nation were crowned in Frankfurt's cathedral.

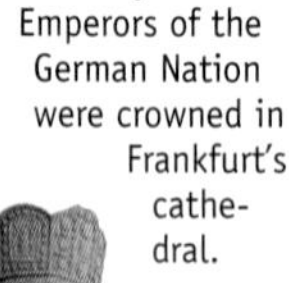

**The Römerberg**
From the "birthplace of German democracy" it is not far to the Römerberg, which has been at the heart of the old quarter since the Middle Ages. At its centre stands the *Gerechtigkeitsbrunnen* (Fountain of Justice), from which wine sometimes flowed rather than water during coronation festivities. From here there is a good view of the building on the west side of the square, which with its characteristic Gothic three-gabled façade is the emblem of the city. The whole town hall complex is called the Römer after the middle house. As the old town hall was no longer adequate for the ceremony of electing kings, in 1405 the city built the Römer and acquired a second house. In the course of time the rambling town hall complex emerged through the purchase of other buildings. However, no part of it is original today, as the entire old quarter with its 2000 timber-framed buildings was destroyed in the Second World War and partly reconstructed after 1945.

The sculptural decoration of the three-gabled façade with its characteristic stepped gables reflects the history of the city and the Holy Roman Empire. The balcony on the upper floor of the Römer is famous: it is used, now as in the past, as the stage for prestigious occasions – although today statesmen or victorious footballers rather than kings are honoured here.

Make a detour to the *Römerhöfchen* in Limpurger Gasse: it has an open spiral stairway dating from 1627, one of the few remaining examples of Renaissance architecture in Frankfurt.

On the ground floor of the *Römer* and the house named *Goldener Schwan* lie the Römerhalle and Schwanenhalle, the oldest surviving rooms in the town hall complex. They were used over centuries for holding trade fairs. In the Kaisersaal on the second floor you have come to a historic site: from 1612 coronation banquets took place here after the election of an emperor. When the room was restored in the 19th century, artists painted life-size portraits of all 52 emperors of the Holy Roman Empire on the walls.

◆ *Kaisersaal 10am–1pm, 2pm–5pm (except during meetings)*

On the east side of the square, timber-framed buildings, erected in the 1980s on the basis of historic models, show how the Römerberg must have appeared in previous centuries.

From the roof gallery of the late Gothic *Alte Nikolaikirche* on the south side of the square, city councillors once had a good view of coronation ceremonies, games or tournaments. Built in the 12th century, this hall church consisting of a nave and single aisle was rebuilt as the church of the council. The figure on the keystone of the nave arch is St Nicholas of Myra, patron of merchants and sailors.

**DomRömer Quarter**
Where once emperors processed from the cathedral to the Römer to celebrate the

coronation ceremony with the people, wealthy patrician families built magnificent houses such as the Renaissance house Zur Goldenen Waage and the inn called Hof zum Rebstock. They were among more than 1200 buildings from all stylistic periods in what was considered, until the bombing raids of 1944, the finest Gothic old quarter in Germany. Demolition of city offices, the Technisches Rathauses, in 1974 made it possible to recreate a small core of 35 Old Town buildings, 15 reconstructed and 20 newly built, and thus to revive the historic coronation way in the new DomRömer Quarter.

*www.domroemer.de*

From here it was not far to the river Main, which was why the guardians of the tower signalled when ships arrived and left. Today the melodies of the 47-part glockenspiel ring out from the tower.

*Römerberg 9*
*◆ 10am-8pm (summer), 10am-6pm (winter)*
*Glockenspiel 9.05am, 12.05pm and 5.05pm*
*www.alte-nikolaikirche.de*

On the left a little further towards the river stands *Haus Wertheim*, the only timber-framed building from the period before 1600 that was spared destruction by bombs. This lane is still called Fahrtor, a name deriving from the medieval gate in the city wall that was once the main entrance to Frankfurt from the river Main. It was defended by the late Gothic Rententurm in the west corner, in which dues and harbour duties were collected. It is part of the Saalhof, the court of the emperor of the Salier dynasty, which now accommodates the *Historisches Museum*.

If you are here during one of its major exhibitions, don't fail to visit the long 1980s building that is clad in travertine stone: the *Schirn Kunsthalle* is one of Germany's leading venues for exhibitions.

*◆ Tue, Fri-Sun 10am-7pm,*
*Wed-Thu 10am-10pm*
*www.schirn.de*

**Dom St. Bartholomäus**

*◆ 10 am-6 pm (April-Oct.),*
*10 am-5 pm (Nov.-March)*

With its 95-metre tower, the imperial cathedral overshadows the entire old quarter. It has never been the seat of a bishop, but the term Kaiserdom ("imperial cathedral") came into use when German

**Frankfurter Kunstverein**
With its projecting towers and crenellations, the Steinernes Haus between the Ostzeile and Technisches Rathaus still catches the eye. When it was built in 1464 for Johann von Melem, a silk merchant from Cologne, this stone Gothic house was unique, surrounded as it was by wooden buildings. Today it is home to the Frankfurter Kunstverein (Art Society), which aims to convey to its visitors the social relevance of contemporary art by means of exhibitions.

*Markt 44*
*◆ Tue, Wed, Fri-Sun*
*11am-7pm*
*Thu 11am-9pm*
*www.fkv.de*

**»Have a break«**

To follow the idyllic halftimbering, the **café bar in the Kunstverein** serves coffee and cake.
◆ *Fri-Wed 10am-7pm*
*Thu 10am-midnight*

kings were elected here from 1356 and Holy Roman emperors were crowned here from 1562.

An inconspicuous sandstone tablet in the ground at the west entrance reveals when the first chapel stood on this spot: it marks the site of a Merovingian child's grave from the period around 680 that lay within the chapel. The present church, with the ground plan of a Greek cross, is the fifth known building to have stood here. It was built in the Gothic period in several phases. It is dedicated to the apostle Bartholomew, who has been the patron saint of the church since 1239.

As a place for coronations, the church naturally holds a wealth of works of art. The Gothic furnishings include the *Maria-Schlaf-Altar* (1434–38) in the Marienkapelle to the north of the choir, which represents the death of the Virgin Mary surrounded by the mourning apostles beneath a richly decorated canopy. In the north transept don't miss Anthony van Dyck's *Deposition from the Cross* of 1627. It was commissioned by the archbishop of Mainz, but when he was unwilling to pay, the painter donated it to a poor monastery.

**Dommuseum**

In the Dommuseum in the medieval former cloister you can find out what possessions were placed into a girl's grave in Merovingian times, see the reliquary in which a relic of St Bartholomew was once kept and admire the treasures that the church accumulated in the course of centuries. The museum presents a chronological tour and holds temporary exhibitions on important historical themes and contemporary art.

◆ *Tue-Fri 10 am-5 pm, Sat-Sun 11 am-5 pm*

*www.dommuseum-frankfurt.de*

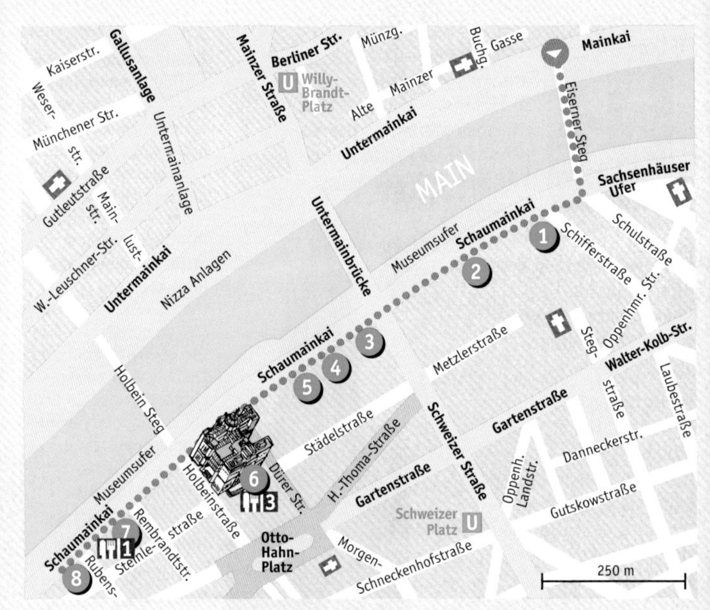


1. Museum für Angewandte Kunst
2. Museum der Weltkulturen
3. Deutsches Filmmuseum
4. Deutsches Architekturmuseum
5. Museum für Kommunikation
6. Städelsches Kunstinstitut
7. Liebieghaus
8. Museum Giersch

1 Café im Liebieghaus
3 Holbein's ➤ p. 37

2 Café Maingold

# Cultural Walks

# CULTURAL WALKS – MUSEUMS ON THE RIVER

*The morning is spent strolling along Germany's unique "Museum Mile", past magnificent villas from past centuries and modern architecture, with a view behind the scenes at the movies before taking a look at some famous sculptures.*

**Eiserner Steg**
You can walk across further proof of the civic spirit of the citizens of Frankfurt by taking the most direct link over the Main between the Römerberg and Sachsenhausen: because Mayor Mumm von Schwarzenstein blocked the citizens' wish for a second bridge, they took it into their own hands and in June 1867 founded a society that financed construction by selling share certificates worth 100 gulden and yielding five per cent interest. Just a year later building work started on the Eiserner Steg, which is 170 metres long and consists of a riveted steel framework with two bridge piers in the river.

**Museumsufer**

The former head of the city cultural department, Hilmar Hoffmann, had the idea of transforming the banks of the Main in Sachsenhausen between the Eiserner Steg and the Friedensbrücke into a mile of culture and art. In the 1980s existing museums were expanded, beautiful patrician villas converted into exhibition spaces, and superb new buildings by international architects constructed. A walk along the Schaumainkai is worthwhile just for the fine architecture.

Beyond the Eiserner Steg is the *Museum für Angewandte Kunst* (Museum of Applied Art, ➤ p. 57) in the park of Villa Metzler. Here Richard Meier's light-flooded design in the shape of three white cubes is integrated into the ensemble of the Neoclassical villa and its park. Past the *Museum der Weltkulturen* (➤ p. 57) and *Filmmuseum* (➤ p. 23) is the spectacular Ein Haus-im-Haus-Entwurf (house-within-a-house) by Matthias Ungers for the *Deutsches Architekturmuseum* (➤ p. 56). In the glass-and-steel building next to the villa of the for-

mer Federal Post Museum, and with a subterranean connection to it, is the seat of the *Museum für Kommunikation* (➤ p. 57). At number 63 the building in historical style with a modern west wing is home to the *Städel* (➤ p. 36), one of Europe's leading art galleries. The villa with turrets and projections, constructed for Baron von Liebieg and now known as the *Liebieghaus*, houses the municipal sculpture collection (➤ p. 25), and the Neoclassical villa is the *Museum Giersch* (➤ p. 57).

**Deutsches Filmmuseum**

*Schaumainkai 41 (Museumsufer)*
▲ *Schweizer Platz*
◆ *Tue, Thu-Sat 10 am-6 pm, Wed 10 am-8 pm*
*www.deutsches-filmmuseum.de*

This museum is not just a treat for real film enthusiasts, but also presents movie history in a way that non-specialists can relate to. On the first floor you can find out about the visual effects and optical illusions that entertained the public in the days before films were invented, and how moving pictures evolved. You can learn about technical apparatus such as the panorama and magic lantern and how they worked, go inside a camera obscura that is directed to the river Main and the Frankfurt skyline, and relive in a reconstruction of the Parisian Grand Café how the Lumière brothers made the first-ever public film projection with their cinematograph on 28 December 1895.

**Hilmar Hoffmann**

No-one has influenced the cultural life of Frankfurt as much as the man who was later president of the Goethe Institut and today presides over the Deutsches Filminstitut/ Filmmuseum. For 20 years, from 1970 to 1990, Hilmar Hoffmann (*1925) was head of the city's cultural affairs, so successfully that, although he is a Social Democrat, he stayed in office under a CDU city government. "Culture for

everyone" was one of his visions, and he worked to establish local libraries and citizens' centres, made his idea of communal cinema into reality in the Filmmuseum, and initiated the rebuilding of the Alte Oper and the Museumsufer.

**Museumsuferfest**
On the last weekend in August each year, over 3 million people flock to the city to celebrate Frankfurt's museums and its river in a three-day festival. In addition to the museum exhibitions, visitors have an opportunity to see the private collections of banks, which are otherwise not open to the public. Food stalls on the promenades on both sides of the river between the Eiserner Steg and Holbeinsteg serve specialities from all round the world, more stalls display arts and crafts as well as other products, and theatres present their programmes of live music, cabaret, variety shows and dance.

*www.museumsuferfest-frankfurt.de*

If you are interested in film as a medium and its production techniques, pass through the scenes made by the film cartoonist George Melies to the second floor of the permanent exhibition, which illuminates every aspect of film production from the pioneering age to the present day. You can discover what the tasks of producers, screenplay authors and directors are, how a film is cut, and how tricks and special effects are employed. In a reconstruction of the set of the legendary Hollywood movie *The Maltese Falcon* (USA 1941) you can take a seat in detective Sam Spade's office and slip into Humphrey Bogart's role, or fly over Frankfurt on a magic carpet thanks to special film effects.

The museum *cinema* is a great attraction. It screens not just retrospectives, documentaries, avant-garde films, premieres and film festivals, but also shows silent movies to the accompaniment of live music from the museum's own Wurlitzer cinema organ, which dates from 1928.

**Liebieghaus – Museum alter Plastik**
*Schaumainkai 71*
▲ *Otto-Hahn-Platz*
◆ *Tue-Wed, Fri-Sun 10am-6pm*
*Thu 10am-9pm*
*www.liebieghaus.de*

When the weather is fine, the idyllic little park of the villa built in 1896 for Baron von Liebieg, a textile manufacturer from Bohemia, is a charming spot to take a rest. Here statues of Athena and Marsyas hint at what is to be found inside the villa: a museum that is among the world's most important for ancient and historic sculpture, telling a 5000-year story from the sculpture of ancient Egypt to the Neoclassical age.

You can find out how the tombs over which the pyramids were built were once decorated, how the burial grounds outside the walls of Athens looked, and what the significance of public spaces was for presenting art in ancient Rome. You will see masterpieces of ancient sculpture, from a *relief from the funeral temple of Sahure* and *Myron's Athena to a portrait of Emperor Marcus Aurelius* and the *Alberici sarcophagus*.

### »Have a break«

For a rest after visiting the museum, the **café** in the courtyard of the Liebieghaus with its home-baked cakes is a wonderful oasis.
*Schaumainkai 71*
◆ *Tue-Sun 10 am-6 pm*

Move on to the Neoclassical room to see what was once Frankfurt's most controversial sculpture, the (naked) figure of *Ariadne on the Panther*, the most famous work of Johann Heinrich von Dannecker. Works such as the *Holy Trinity* by Hans Multscher show that politics, everyday life and Christianity were inseparably bound together in the Middle Ages. Antico's bronze statue of *Apollo Belvedere* demonstrates how the formal language of antiquity inspired Renaissance artists, and Matthias Steinl's *Maria Immaculata* takes you to the Baroque era before you ascend to the upper floor and the so-called *bozetti*, sculptors' studies made of a variety of materials. Finally, on the top floor you can learn what a studiolo is: a room for studying the arts.

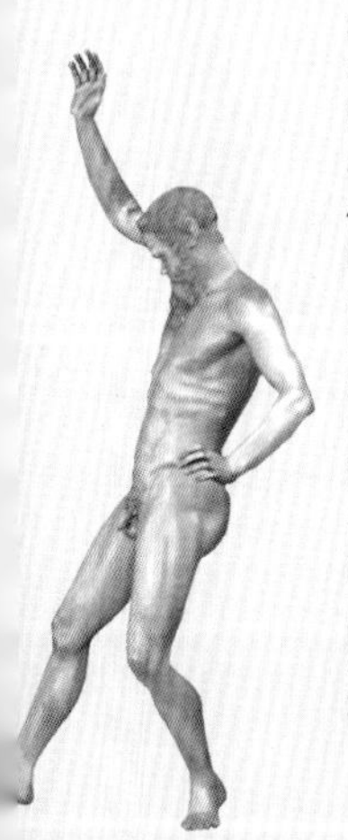

**A breath of the Mediterranean ...**

... is in the air on the opposite bank of the Main: on the 800-metre strip between Untermain and the Friedensbrücke over 150 species of southern European plants grow in the shelter of the quayside walls and in sunlight reflected from the river. Palms, lemon and fig trees, plane trees, cedars and even a gingko tree flourish in the so-called Nizza-Gärten (Gardens of Nice), which were planted between 1866 and 1875 and thanks to their Mediterranean atmosphere are a favourite place to linger for the people of Frankfurt.

# STROLLING AND SHOPPING – CITY CENTRE, AIRPORT & CO

*Armani, chocolate or lifestyle, tailor-made or prêt-a-porter, Frankfurt has many places where you can shop to your heart's content.*

**City centre**
If you stroll along the *Zeil* from Konstablerwache to Hauptwache, you are on the shopping street with the highest turnover in Germany, where large department and fashion stores, branches of international chains and unusual shops such as those of Adidas and Puma tempt you to go on a spree, or at least window-shopping.

Don't fail to take a look inside the mall named *My Zeil*, the work of the Italian star architect Massimiliano Fuksas (Zeil 106), if only for its spectacular architecture and futuristic roof design. Here you can also go shopping on eight floors to find whatever you desire, and ride on Europe's longest unsupported escalator!

For a contrast take a detour into the *Kleinmarkthalle* (little market hall) at Hasengasse 5–7: the city's favourite food market occupies the site where Germany's oldest market hall once stood.

*»Have a break«*
For a stop between the shops, try the **Café Maingold.**
*Zeil 1 ◆ Mon-Thu noon-1am, Fri-Sat noon-2am, Sun 10am-9pm*

**Rosemarie Nitribitt**
Despite enormous media interest, a novel and two films, little is known for certain about the life of a woman whose emblem was a black Mercedes 190 with red leather seats and a white poodle. In the oh-so-prudish age when Adenauer was West German chancellor in the 1950s, the high-class prostitute Rosemarie Nitribitt was a well-known personality in Frankfurt. An

illegitimate child, she grew up in humble circumstances and did everything she could to compensate for her lack of education and manners – successfully, as her clientele included renowned politicians and businessmen. That was why her murder on 1 November 1957 became the biggest sex scandal of the post-war era. To this day the case remains unsolved.

The so-called "calory exchange" sells everything from fresh fruit and vegetables, cheese, sausage and bread to exotic specialities.

If you like to admire the creations of leading designers, walk a little further towards the Alte Oper and into *Goethestrasse*, which is regarded as Frankfurt's Fifth Avenue. Here you will find boutiques of all the big names, from Armani to Zegna. Lovers of good food head for Grosse Bockenheimer Strasse, also known as *Fressgass* ("eat street"), where many delicatessens have set up store.

**Outside the centre**
Some of the shopping streets in quarters outside the city centre are also attractive. Berger Strasse, for example, in the district of *Bornheim*, has lots of little shops, cafés and pubs that make it one of the most popular places to go strolling and shopping. The market held there on Wednesdays and Saturdays around the clock tower is one of the nicest in Frankfurt.

*Hanauer Landstrasse* is the haunt of night owls, but appeals not only to them. For those who are interested in cars or hunting for a designer bargain or two, this traffic artery in a former industrial area has lots of factory outlets and automobile brands.

In the Sachsenhausen district you can go window-shopping past up-market boutiques and specialist stores in *Schweizer Strasse*, which is very close to the Museumsufer. *Brückenstrasse* is home to a trendy scene: here you will find interesting design stores mixed up with shops selling everyday items.

**Airport Shopping**
Frankfurt Airport is a shopper's paradise: stores are open there 365 days a year, including Sundays and holidays and in many cases until late in the evening. And more than 60 million passengers a year, plus numerous visitors and the 81,000 people who work at the airport, take advantage of these opportunities day in and day out. Shopping at the airport is made even more attractive by the colorful mix of international stores, major brands and regional highlights. There are also numerous food and beverage outlets ranging from cafés across small eateries to gourmet restaurants. Travelers can find real bargains at tax- and duty-free prices in 22 Duty Free and Travel Value shops. All this adds up to an exciting shopping experience at an extraordinary location with a unique atmosphere!

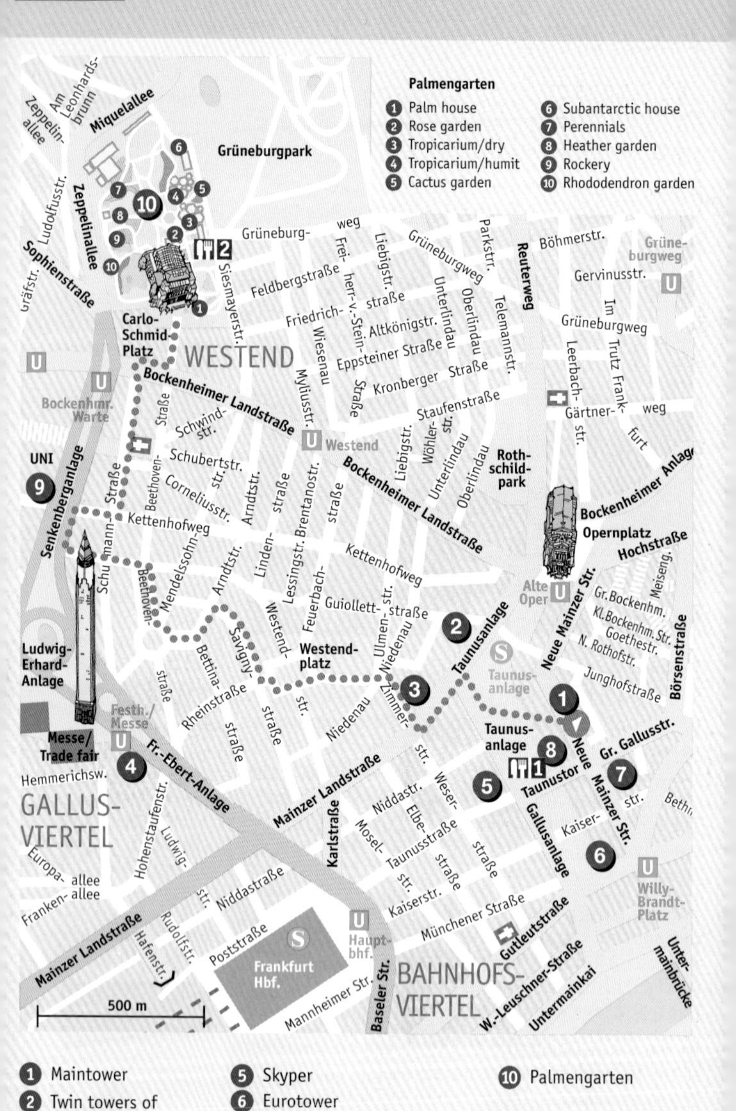


1 Maintower
2 Twin towers of Deutsche Bank
3 Trianon
4 Castor and Pollux
5 Skyper
6 Eurotower
7 Commerzbank Tower
8 Japan Center
9 Naturmuseum Senckenberg
10 Palmengarten

Restaurant 1 Unser Täglich Brot
Restaurant 2 Café Siesmayer
Restaurant 3 Holbein´s ➤ map p. 20

Day 3

# Art and Money

# THE WESTEND – BANKS, SKYSCRAPERS AND PALMS

*Today you can take a look at the Frankfurt skyline from up close before you meet a tyrannosaurus rex, walk through all the earth's vegetation zones and discover interesting plants such as the mother-in-law's armchair and the screw tree.*

**Anlagenring**
Where once the fortified city wall stood, today a green belt about five kilometres long with leafy walks, ponds, fountains and monuments surrounds the city centre. As Frankfurt kept expanding beyond its old boundaries, and the fortifications had become obsolete in military terms, the walls and gates were torn down in the early 19th century and the site, a strip between 50 and 100 metres wide, was made into a park. Its different sections are named after the city gates that once stood there, of which only the late Gothic Eschenheimer Turm has survived.

## Mainhattan

Can you imagine that the Kaiserdom at 96 metres height was the tallest building in Frankfurt until the 1950s? When you look towards it today from the other side of the Main, you see almost 100 skyscrapers. Along with the church towers in the foreground, they dominate the city skyline, and by way of comparison with Manhattan in New York have given Frankfurt the nickname *Mainhattan*.

Many skyscrapers are concentrated in the banking district, where numerous German and European banks have their headquarters. And so you start the day with a little bit of Wall Street atmosphere and experience something of the bankers' lifestyle on Neue Mainzer Strasse: people dressed in dark business clothing who hurry from one office block to another and maybe make a brief stop in one of the coffee bars, but always with a mobile phone at their ear and a laptop or netbook at the ready: time is money!

Understandably, the buildings are not open to the public – with one exception, the *Maintower* at number 52, at 200 metres the fourth-tallest skyscraper in Frankfurt and an architectural masterpiece. It consists of two buildings nested into one another: a square one 170 metres high, and a round one with a height of 199.5 metres, with the façade of the previous building on the site, a protected

monument, integrated into the base. When it was completed in 1999 it was the first skyscraper in Europe to have a façade entirely of glass. Here you can take a lift to the viewing platform on the 54th floor for a panorama of the whole city and its architecturally impressive high-rises.

*Neue Mainzer Strasse 52*
*◆ Summer: Sun-Thu 10am-9pm, Fri-Sat 10am-11pm, winter: Sun-Thu 10am-7pm, Fri-Sat 10am-9pm*

An eye-catching feature of the Frankfurt skyline are the fully refurbished towers of Deutsche Bank, known as Soll and Haben (Debit and Credit), with reflecting glass façades that appear either cool or glowing according to the sunlight and are now among the world's most environmentally friendly skyscrapers. The *Trianon* (1993), headquarters of the Deka Bank, rises to the heavens in the shape of an equilateral triangle, its corners also formed from triangular towers, and with an inverted three-sided pyramid of glass on the roof.

The two towers at the trade fair that make up the office complex known as the Forum are named *Castor* (95 metres) and *Pollux* (126 metres) after the twins of Greek mythology. Next to them the *Messeturm* (trade fair tower, 1990), one of the emblems of the city, is reminiscent of American skyscraper architecture of the 1920s with its structure, increasingly slender as it rises, of base, tower and pinnacle. Further away on the trade fair grounds is Oswald Matthias Ungers' *Torhaus* (gateway, 1984) in the shape of two interpenetrating cubes. On the banks of the Main stands the *Westhafen Tower* (2003). Its glass façade with a diamond

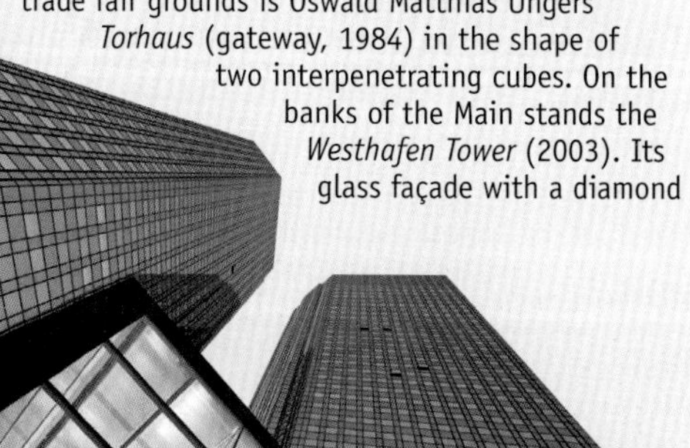

**Financial centre**
Share prices, base interest rates, financial trends – in no city in Germany are financial themes discussed more than in Frankfurt. All important financial and business institutions are represented in the city. 201 banks, over half of them foreign, are based in Frankfurt. The European Central Bank and the Asian Development Bank have their headquarters here, and the European and German branches of national banks are also present. Investment companies in Frankfurt manage 80 per cent of the total assets of German funds, and 90 per cent of German stock market turnover takes place here. The watchdog of the bank system is BaFin, the federal institution for supervising financial services.

**IG-Farben-Haus**
On part of the university site known as Campus Westend stands a building that looks like an office block and was still regarded as highly modern in the 1950s. The nine-storey building clad in travertine stone with six wings linked by a central lobby was built in 1928–31 by Hans Poelzig as the headquarters of the IG Farben company. When IG Farben, the world's largest chemical company, was split up due to its involvement with the Nazi regime, the building became the headquarters of the US occupying force and the scene of historic events: in 1948 the constitution of the state of Hesse was signed and the Basic Law of the Federal Republic was commissioned in General Eisenhower's office.

pattern looks like a glass for apple wine and has given it the nickname "Gerippter" or "Äppelwoi-Turm". Closer, near to *Gallileo* (2003) and the *Silvertower* (1978) in the banking district, stands the 154-metre *Skyper* (2004), which is connected by a nine-metre-high hall of glass to a protected monument dating from 1915, once the imposing villa of the Holzmann company. Nearer to you on Willy-Brandt-Platz the European Central Bank had its seat in the *Eurotower* until 2014, as the large Euro sculpture in front still reveals.

At 259 metres the *Commerzbank Tower* (1997) by Sir Norman Foster, one of Europe's tallest buildings, set new a benchmark in architecture: individual blocks of eight storeys each have been hung onto an outer framework of three corner buildings, thus creating a 160-metre-high atrium as the inner core. Air is supplied to the tower by four-storey conservatories, three on each side, in which Mediterranean, Asian or American plants are grown, depending on which direction they face.

With its Asian-influenced architecture, projecting roof and stone cladding in the colour of terracotta, the *Japan Center* (1996) is a distinctive element on the skyline.

*»Have a break«*
For a freshly baked roll to keep you going, try **Unser täglich Brot** on the ground floor of the Japan-Tower.
*Taunustor 2 ◆ Mon-Fri 7am-5pm*

**Westend**
Following the green belt, this walk goes along Taunusanlage through the Westend, one of the city's most attractive residential areas with its fine villas and houses of the late 19th and early 20th centuries.

**Naturmuseum Senckenberg**
Senckenberganlage 25
(Bockenheim)
▲ *Bockenheimer Warte*
◆ *Mon, Tue, Thu-Fri 9am-5pm,*
*Wed 9am-8pm, Sat-Sun 9am-6pm*
*www.senckenberg.de*

At the end of Taunusanlage a historic museum building accommodates one of Germany's largest collections on natural history. Here you can learn how life forms have evolved and how the earth has changed over millions of years. Even if you have come to Frankfurt without children, the dinosaurs on the ground floor are a must! The 18 species on display are the most extensive collection in Germany, and you can learn to tell the difference between a diplodocus, triceratops and a tyrannosaurus rex.

The dinosaurs are just a tiny part of the collection of extinct animals, an introduction to life in different geological eras. An anaconda swallowing a capybara pig, a gigantic finback whale, a primeval seed-bearing plant called moresnetia and a cast of the skeleton of Lucy, who lived three million years ago in what is now Ethiopia – all these are part of a visitor-friendly presentation of the earth's history on three floors.

The Geopark takes you on stroll through geological time: large-scale displays including living fossils such as gingkos and redwoods, a dinosaur's footprint and a replica of a sigillaria tree from the Carboniferous period illustrate the natural world in different eras.

**Höchst**
A district of Frankfurt that is known for its chemicals plant and for the porcelain factory of the same name originated in a small Roman fort. However Höchst, which was granted a municipal charter as early as 1355–56, also has a picturesque old quarter with winding lanes, half-timbered houses and a Gothic customs tower. It is also worth visiting the church of St Justus with its Carolingian nave and High Gothic choir. The landmark of Höchst is the Gothic keep of the Renaissance castle, today home to a museum on the history of Höchst and the Hoechst AG company museum.

**Heinrich Siesmayer**
Like so many projects in Frankfurt, the Palmengarten arose from the initiative of a private citizen.

## Palmengarten

*Siesmayerstrasse 61*
▲ *Bockenheimer Warte*
◆ *9am-6pm (Feb-Oct), 9am-4pm (Nov-Jan)*
*www.palmengarten.de*

When the Free Imperial City of Frankfurt and Hesse-Nassau came under Prussian rule and Duke Adolf von Nassau gave up his ducal residence in 1866, the tropical trees and plants in the orangery of Schloss Biebrich went on sale. This gave Heinrich Siesmayer, a garden expert, the opportunity to carry out his idea of establishing a house for tropical plants. The Palmengarten society, financed by the issue of shares, was founded in May 1869, and a mere two years later was able to inaugurate the *Palmengarten*, which Siesmayer designed, on 16 March 1871.

Frankfurt's best-known park is by no means devoted to palm trees alone! Here you can see plants from all over the world – from rainforest jungle to hot and humid mangrove swamps and arid desert landscapes. You can visit hothouses, walk through themed gardens past little fountains and ponds and lie down to sunbathe on the lawns.

A circuit of the park starts just behind the main entrance at the historic *palm house* of 1869, which adjoins the building of the founding society, the Palmengarten-Gesellschaft. With a length of 52 metres and a width of 30 metres it is one of the largest of its kind in Europe. The citizens of Frankfurt are specially proud of the Chinese hemp-palms near the entrance, which are survivors from when the Palmengarten was founded. The interior is a luxuriant subtropical scene with great palm trees, giant perennials, tree ferns and other leafy plants.

Several aquariums in a grotto-like underpass provide a glimpse of the colourful undersea world of the tropics. Next to them it is worth taking a look at the *gallery*, which stages interesting exhibitions all year round. On the right is the *historic show-house* dating from 1905, where you can find out about carnivorous plants and tillandsia.

From here continue to the *rose garden*, which was laid out in 1886 in strictly geometric forms as a classical rose parterre, an interplay of flower beds, lawns and paths. Here you can learn to tell the difference between fragrant roses and "old" roses.

An attractive place in summer is the *cactus garden* with succulents and flowering plants that are native to America, Africa and the Canary Isles. Next stop is the *Tropicarium*, a computer-controlled complex consisting of seven large and six smaller hothouses that are one of the highlights of the Palmengarten, demonstrating the variety of tropical habitats and the diverse forms of their plants.

The *subantarctic house* displays the flora of the cool and temperate zones of the southern hemisphere with plants from New Zealand and Patagonia. Don't on any account miss the *Blütenhaus* (house of blooms) at the nursery, a great sea of colour covering an area of 200 square metres at all times of the year. Numerous gardens such as the colourful heather garden, the rockery with its impressive waterfall and the magnificent rhododendron garden also tempt visitors to linger.

*»Have a break«*

If the garden gives you an appetite, to go **Café Siesmayer** for wonderful cakes, home-made ice cream and filling snacks.

◆ *8am-7pm*

**Festival of Roses and Light**

One of Frankfurt's finest festivals, the Rosen- und Lichterfest, is held each June, when a big exhibition in the Palmengarten celebrates the queen of flowers. Visitors can then admire blooming roses at their leisure and learn all about these flowers. A wide-ranging programme of guided walks, theatre, dance and live music complements the exhibition and reaches its climax on the Saturday evening, when tea candles are lit to create pictures all over the garden and a superb firework display is set off at the boating pond.

## STÄDEL MUSEUM – SEVEN CENTURIES OF PAINTING

*Whether you prefer late medieval panel painting, Baroque landscapes, portraits or still-lifes, the Städel Museum invites you to take a journey through the centuries.*

**Städel**
*Schaumainkai 63 (Sachsenhausen)*
▲ *Schweizer Platz*
◆ *Tue-Wed, Sat-Sun 10am-6pm, Thu-Fri 10am-9pm*
*www.staedelmuseum.de*

A garden full of plants and flowers, a lady absorbed in a book, a child making music, men singing – it looks like a scene at court in a palace grounds, and it was chosen early in the 15th century by the Oberrheinischer Meister (master of the Upper Rhine) to set the scene for a depiction of the heavenly paradise with the Virgin Mary and the Christ Child surrounded by saints. This "hortus conclusus" was regarded at that time as a symbol of the immaculate nature of the Virgin.

The *Paradise Garden* is just one of many masterpieces in the collection. The best place to begin is the second floor, where works from the 14th to the 18th century are exhibited. Here you can see Jan van Eyck's *Lucca Madonna*, Lucas Cranach's *Venus* and Sandro Botticelli's *Idealised Portrait of a Lady*: the Italian Renaissance and old masters from Germany and the Netherlands are equally well represented. Jan Vermeer's *Geographer* and *The Blinding of Simon* by Rembrandt are just two of the highlights in the Baroque rooms.

The best-known painting in the Städel, certainly for German art lovers, is to be found on the first floor – even though the proportions are not right and it depicts two left feet. It portrays Frankfurt's most famous son sitting on an obelisk with a flat landscape of ruins and the Alban Hills in the background.

**Städelsches Kunstinstitut and Städelschule**

For its status today as owner of one of the world's leading galleries of paintings, the city of Frankfurt is indebted to the merchant and banker Johann Friedrich Städel (1728–1816), who had collected about 500 paintings, mostly by Flemish, Dutch and German artists of the 17th and 18th centuries, and 2000 engravings and drawings by the time he died. As Städel, who never married and had no children, wished to keep his collection together and make it available to his fellow citizens, in his will he left his wealth for the establishment of a public art collection and a school of art.

Tischbein's *Goethe in the Roman Campagna* came to the museum in 1887 as a gift from the Rothschild family. It became the best-known portrait of the poet and has influenced our conception of Goethe's appearance to this day.

This is the starting point for a journey through the art of the 19th and 20th centuries that provides encounters with currents in German painting: the Romantic movement is exemplified by Caspar David Friedrich's *Landscape with Rosenberg*, the Biedermeier period by Spitzweg's *Lover of Roses*, Realism by Wilhelm Leibl's *Elderly Farmer and Young Girl* and Expressionism by Ernst Ludwig Kirchner's *Varieté*. French Realism is represented by Courbet's *Wave*, and Impressionism by paintings such as Degas' *Orchestra Musicians* and Manet's *Croquet Party*.

Picasso's *Portrait of Fernande Olivier* is an example of the Cubist style, Paul Klee's *Fertile Country* an early abstract painting. Contemporary art has been given an unusual location, with a new exhibition hall beneath the Städel garden and its significant circular skylights: paintings from East and West make for a unique journey of discovery through the history of art since 1945.

*»Have a break«* 3

If you can take your eyes off the paintings, there is excellent food in **Holbein's** café-restaurant.

*Holbeinstrasse 1*

◆ *Tue-Sun 10am-midnight*

**The Rothschilds**

There is hardly a better-known name in the world of finance, and in the 19th century there was hardly a more influential family than the Rothschilds, whose home was the Judengasse (Jews' Alley). The founder of the dynasty, the money-changer Mayer Amschel Rothschild (1744–1812), laid the foundations for the family bank through astute financial transactions with the prince elector during the turbulent period of the Napoleonic Wars. After his death, his five sons took over the company and financed everything from railways to the Suez Canal. In just two decades the bank became a leading European finance house, and today has more than 50 branches in 30 countries on five continents.

*www.rothschild.com*

Service

# Hotels

*Whether your are looking for a top-class address, a design hotel or a modern business hotel, whether near the banking quarter, the trade fair or the airport, there is a wide range of accommodation in Frankfurt.*

**Frankfurt Trade Fair**
With a surface of 592,000 square metres, ten halls with an area of 366.637 square metres and a further 96,078 square metres of open ground, the grounds of Messe Frankfurt in the districts Bockenheim and Westend-Süd are the world's third-largest trade fair. Each year around 43,000 exhibitors present themselves to 1.6 million visitors at 51 trade fairs and exhibitions. With nearly 150 congresses and conventions, Messe Frankfurt is also one of Europe's leading congress destinations.

*www.messefrankfurt.com*

■ **Art-Hotel Robert Mayer*****
Robert-Mayer-Strasse 44
60486 Frankfurt
(Bockenheim)
Tel. 069/9709100
Fax 069/97091010
▲ Adabert-Schlossstrasse, Frankfurt-West
*www.arthotel-frankfurt.de*

Design hotel in a 100-year-old villa, a protected monument near the trade fair and university in which each room was individually styled by an artist.

■ **Bristol Hotel Frankfurt******
Ludwigstrasse 15
60327 Frankfurt
(near main station)
Tel. 069/242390
Fax 069/251539
▲ Festhalle/Messe, Platz der Republik
*www.bristol-hotel.de*

Design hotel managed by the owner with an out-of-the-ordinary interior and regular events. The summer lounge, among Japanese parasols and bamboo, is a wonderful spot for breakfast and more.

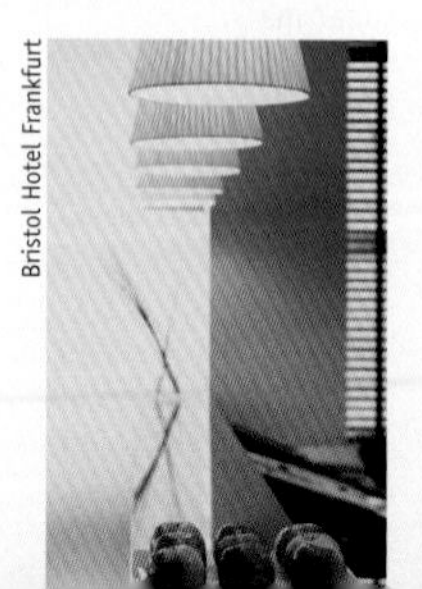
Bristol Hotel Frankfurt

■ **Goldmann 25Hours******
Hanauer Landstrasse 127
60314 Frankfurt (Ostend)
Tel. 069/40586890
Fax 069/4058689890
▲ Ostbahnhof, Osthafenplatz
*www.25hours-hotels.com*

Was recently voted the best hotel under 100 € in Europe. Every room tells its own story.

■ **Hilton Frankfurt Hotel******
Hochstrasse 4
60313 Frankfurt
(city centre)
Tel. 069/133800
Fax 069/133820
▲ Eschersheimer Tor
*www3.hilton.com*

An oasis in the heart of the city. The modern Hilton in a park right next to the stock exchange has one of Frankfurt's loveliest park terraces as well as lots of space to relax in the semi-Olympic pool.

■ **Leonardo Royal Hotel Frankfurt******
Mailänder Strasse 1
60598 Frankfurt
(Sachsenhausen)
Tel. 069/68020
Fax 069/68020333
▲ Südfriedhof
*www.leonardo-hotels.de*

This centrally located 4-star hotel, one of the city's first skyscrapers, occupies the highest point in the Sachsenhausen residential area with a wonderful view the city skyline.

Radisson Blu Hotel

■ **Hotel Beethoven******
Beethovenstrasse 46
60325 Frankfurt (Westend)
Tel. 069/7434970
Fax 069/748466
▲ Bockenheimer Warte
*www.hotelbeethoven.de*

Comfortable hotel in a beautifully restored old villa near the trade fair, university and banking quarter.

■ **Hotel Cult****
Offenbacher Landstrasse 56
60599 Frankfurt (Sachsenhausen)
Tel. 069/9624460
Fax 069/962446666
▲ Lokalbahnhof
*www.hotelcult.de*

Stylish business hotel from which the trade fair, banking district and shopping areas are in easy reach.

■ **Hotel Nizza*****
Elbestrasse 10
60329 Frankfurt (near main station)
Tel. 069/2425380
Fax 069/24253830
▲ Hauptbahnhof
*www.hotelnizza.de*

Once but no longer a well-kept secret for actors, artists and performers: a small, intimate hotel with no interior frills but a roof garden and a skyline panorama.

■ **Hotel Villa Orange*****
Hebelstrasse 1
60318 Frankfurt (Nordend)
Tel. 069/405840
Fax 069/40584100
▲ Musterschule
*www.villa-orange.de*

Small, ecologically certified business hotel with a historic façade, just 5 minutes from the Zeil.

■ **InterCityHotel Frankfurt Airport*****
Am Luftbrückendenkmal 1
60549 Frankfurt (airport)
Tel. 069/697099
Fax 069/69709555
▲ Flughafen
*www.intercityhotel.com*

Modern hotel with all amenities at the airport.

■ **Le Méridien Parkhotel Frankfurt*******
Wiesenhüttenplatz 28–38
60329 Frankfurt (near main station)
Tel. 069/26970
Fax 069/2697884
▲ Hauptbahnhof
*www.lemeridienparkhotelfrankfurt.com*

Here you can enjoy the luxurious charm of a grand hotel, right next to the banking and business district.

**The Visitors' Terrace at Frankfurt Airport**

If you are interested in inhaling the scent of the big wide world at Germany's largest airport, the Visitors' Terrace in Terminal 2 is ideal. The entrance is in the Food Plaza opposite McDonald's on Level 4. It provides an excellent vantage point for watching the activity out on the apron and airfield. Each year, Frankfurt Airport welcomes more than 60 million passengers to its two terminals. Around 1300 planes land and take off daily. With 100 airlines serving some 300 destinations in about a hundred countries and a yearly airfreight volume of 2.11 million tonnes, it is one of the world's most important air transportation hubs.

*www.visitorsterrace.frankfurt-airport.com/en*

# Hotels

**Goethe University**
In 1914, thanks to the initiative of many citizens of Frankfurt, Germany's first university to be established by a foundation opened under the distinguished name Johann Wolfgang Goethe-Universität. Since then many Nobel Prize laureates, such as Paul Ehrlich (medicine), Hans Bethe (physics) and Günter Grass (literature), have studied or taught here. Today, with more than 46,000 students, over 640 professors and 170 courses, it is one of the Germany´s five largest universities. 16 faculties are divided between sites at Bockenheim, Riedberg, Westend and Niederrad, and in time for the 100th anniversary a new campus will open around the IG-Farben-Haus.

*www.uni-frankfurt.de*

■ **Maritim Hotel*****\
Theodor-Heuss-Allee 3
60486 Frankfurt (trade fair)
Tel. 069/75780
Fax 069/75781000
▲ Festhalle/Messe, Ludwig-Erhard-Anlage
*www.maritim.de*

High-class hotel next to the trade fair site with a wonderful pool above the roofs of Frankfurt.

■ **Marriot Frankfurt******
Hamburger Allee 2–10
60486 Frankfurt (Bockenheim)
Tel. 069/79550
Fax 069/79552432
▲ Festhalle Messe
*www.marriott.de*

The largest business hotel and the tallest hotel on the continent, opposite the trade fair and close to the congress centre with a panoramic view over Frankfurt and its surroundings.

■ **Mövenpick Hotel Frankfurt City******
Den Haager Strasse 5
60327 Frankfurt (trade fair)
Tel. 069/7880750
Fax 069/788075888
▲ Festhalle/Messe
*www.moevenpick-frankfurt-city.com*

An excellent address for business travellers, visitors to the trade fair and weekenders. It lies right opposite Messe Frankfurt, and you can relax on the roof terrace with a view of the city skyline.

■ **Radisson Blu Hotel******
Franklinstrasse 65
60486 Frankfurt (Bockenheim)
Tel. 069/7701550
Fax 069/77015510
▲ Westbahnhof, An der Dammweide
*www.radissonblu.de/hotel-frankfurt*

4-star-superior hotel near the trade fair site with remarkable architecture in the shape of a standing disc. The interior was created by the Italian star designer Matteo Thun.

■ **Sheraton Frankfurt Hotel & Towers, Conference Center*******
Flughafen Terminal 1, Hugo-Eckener-Ring 15
60549 Frankfurt (airport)
Fax 069/69772209
▲ Flughafen
*www.sheratonfrankfurtairport.com*

As a meeting place at the hub of Europe, a stopover on a journey or the starting point for a trip into the city, this modern hotel at the airport provides every luxury and excellent transport connections.

Goldmann 25Hours

Villa Orange

■ **Steigenberger Frankfurter Hof*****
Am Kaiserplatz 1
60311 Frankfurt
(city centre)
Tel. 069/21502
Fax 069/215900
▲ Willy-Brandt-Platz
*www.steigenberger.com*

The classic grand address in Frankfurt, an old-established luxury hotel right in the city centre that combines bygone splendour with modern comfort.

■ **The Pure****
Niddastrasse 86
60329 Frankfurt
(near main station)
Tel. 069/7104570
Fax 069/710457177
▲ Festhalle/Messe, Platz der Republik
*www.the-pure.de*

One of Germany's most original design hotels, housed in a five-storey 19th-century loft, in minimalist design and purist white.

■ **The Westin Grand Frankfurt*****
Konrad-Adenauer-Strasse 7
60313 Frankfurt
(city centre)
Tel. 069/29810
Fax 069/2981810
▲ Konstablerwache
*www.westingrandfrankfurt.com*

Close to the Zeil shopping street, this luxurious hotel is a perfect base for business travellers or holiday-makers in the city of banks.

Maritim Hotel

■ **Villa Kennedy*****
Kennedyallee 70
60596 Frankfurt
(Sachsenhausen)
Tel. 069/717120
Fax 069/717122000
▲ Stresemannallee/Gartenstrasse
*www.villakennedy.com*

Luxury accommodation in a magnificent early 20th-century villa near the museum district.

Zoologischer Garten Frankfurt

**Frankfurt Zoo**
A stroll through Germany's second-oldest zoo is like a journey of discovery to all the world's continents, taking in 500 different species and over 4500 animals. Go inside Europe's largest house for nocturnal animals, which is named after the zoo's former director, Bernhard Grzimek. Don't miss the Borgori Forest with its primates – Frankfurt Zoo has a worldwide reputation for breeding them. The big cat jungle with its Indian lions, Sumatra tigers and rusty-spotted cats is another highlight. And if you have always wanted to experience a tropical storm, pay a visit to the Exotarium.

Bernhard-Grzimek-Allee 1 (Ostend)
▲ Zoo
◆ 9am-7pm (summer), 9am-5pm (winter)

*www.zoo-frankfurt.de*

# Cafes and Lunch

*For gateau, green-tea cake, pancake or pasta, in a salon, a Viennese coffee house or on the terrace, in Frankfurt there are many reasons and places for taking a break.*

### Frankfurt Calendar

**January**
★ Christmasworld: *christmasworld. messefrankfurt.com*

**February**
★ Frankfurt Carnival: *www.grosser-rat.de/ fastnachtszug*

**March**
★ International Music Fair: *musik.messefrankfurt.com*
★ Luminale (every second year): *www.luminale-frankfurt.de*

**April**
★ Frühjahrs-Dippemess: *www.dippemess.de*

**May**
★ Festival on Fressgass: *www.frankfurt.de*
★ Museum Night: *www.nacht-der-museen.de*
★ Nippon Connection: *www.nipponconnection.com*

**June:**
★ Palace Festival in Höchst: *www.pro-hoechst.de/ hoechster-schlossfest*
★ Festival on Opern-platz: *www.opernplatzfest.com*
★ Parade of Cultures (every second year): *parade-der-kulturen.de*
★ Festival of Roses and Lights: *www.palmengarten.de*
★ Wäldchestag: *www.dippemess.de*

**■ Bitter & Zart**
Chocolaterie & Salon
Braubachstr. 14
▲ Dom/Römer
◆ Mon-Sat 10am-7pm, Sun 11am-6pm

Whether you opt for the famous chocolate cake, a fruit tart, a sandwich with caramelised pear and brie, or coffee, tea, cocoa or some bubbly, you'll go weak at the knees here.

**■ Buch-Café im Jüdischen Museum**
Untermainkai 14/15
(city centre)
▲ Willy-Brandt-Platz
◆ Tue 10am-8pm,
Wed-Sun 10am-6pm

Here you can drink coffee and browse books. The café with bookshop attached also frequently holds interesting readings.

**■ Café Laumer**
Bockenheimer Landstrasse 67 (Westend)
▲ Westend
◆ 8am-7pm

The philosopher Adorno used to enjoy the cakes here.

**■ Café Metropol**
Weckmarkt 13-15
(City)
▲ Dom/Römer
◆ Tue-Sun 9am-1pm

Classic coffee house with a colourful mix of customers, serving light meals as well as home-made cakes.

**■ Café Wacker**
Kornmarkt 9-11 (Bornheim)
▲ Bornheim Mitte
◆ Mon-Fri 8am-7pm,
Sat 8am-6pm

One of the most attractive coffee houses in Frankfurt. Beans have been roasted on the premises since 1914.

**■ Eiscafè Fontanella**
Kaiserstraße 36 (City)
▲ Willy-Brandt-Platz
◆ 9.30 am-10 pm

Traditional Italian ice-cream parlour with delicious flavours that are created in-house.

**■ Espressionist**
Friedrich-Ebert-Anlage 35-37
south side Tower 185
▲ Festhalle/Messe
◆ Mon-Fri 8am-6pm,
Sat 10am-6pm

Harveys

A cosy coffee bar near to the trade fair grounds where visitors can breakfast with colleagues or business partners over an excellent espresso or filtered coffee.

■ **Goldmund im Literaturhaus**
Schöne Aussicht 2 (Ostend)
▲ Hospital zum Heiligen Geist
◆ Mon-Fri 11-midnight, Sat 6pm- midnight

In summer the inviting garden has shady spots under the plane trees, while the restaurant turns out modern interpretations of proper old-fashioned cooking.

■ **Harveys**
Bornheimer Landstrasse 64 (Nordend)
▲ Friedberger Platz
◆ Mon-Fri 9am-1am, Sat 9am-2am, Sun 9am-midnight

Breakfast is served here until 4pm. Other dishes can be enjoyed on the pleasant terrace.

■ **Ilmori Patisserie**
Braubachstrasse 24 (Innenstadt)
▲ Römer, Merianplatz
◆ Mon-Fri 9am-9pm, Sat-Sun 10am-9pm

Something different: this Japanese coffee house with Viennese charm serves green-tea cake and rolls with sweet bean paste, but also French patisserie products.

■ **MainNizza**
Untermainkai 17 (city centre)
▲ Willy-Brandt-Platz
◆ 11.30-1am

For a quick but good business lunch or a fine dinner in a modern glass cube with a wonderful outdoor terrace, Nizza brings a touch of Mediterranean feeling to the river Main.

■ **Medici**
Weissadlergasse 2 (city centre)
▲ Hauptwache
◆ Mon-Sat from 11am

A tip for lovers of fine food, not just at lunchtime. Medici serves high-class cooking at reasonable prices.

■ **Souper! Die Suppenküche.**
Weissadlergasse 3 (city centre)
▲ Hauptwache
◆ Mon-Sat 11.30am-6pm

Whether you prefer gazpacho, Thai coconut chicken or cream of tomato soup with mozzarella, this is the place for soup, fresh daily.

## *Frankfurt Calendar*

**July**
★ Mainova IRONMAN European Championship: *eu.ironman.com*
★ Osthafen-Festival: *www.osthafenfestival.de*
★ Street Festival of Schweizer Strasse: *www.die-schweizerstrasse.de*

**August**
★ Apple Wine Festival: *www.frankfurt.de*
★ Mainfest: *www.dippemess.de*
★ Museumsufer Festival: *www.museumsuferfest.de*

**September**
★ Herbst-Dippemess (funfair): *www.dippemess.de*
★ International Motor Show (every second year): *www.iaa.de*
★ Rheingau Wine Market: *www.frankfurt-tourismus.de*
★ Fountain Festival of Sachsenhausen: *brunnenfest-sachsenhausen.de*

**October**
★ German Jazz Festival: *jazzfestival.hr2-kultur.de*
★ Frankfurt Book Fair: *www.buchmesse.de*
★ LUCAS International Festival for Young Filmlovers: *lucas-filmfestival.de*

**December**
★ Christmas markets: *www.frankfurt-tourismus.de*

# Restaurants

*Paté de foie gras or pizza, regional Hessian cooking or crossover, gourmet destinations or bistros, Frankfurt has a wide choice of restaurants that invite visitors to take a trip through all the tastes of the world.*

## Frankfurt specialities

**Apfelwein:** a fruit wine but not sweet, containing about 5.5–7 per cent alcohol, usually pressed and fermented from a mix of various kinds of apples with as much acidity as possible.

**Brenten:** a sweet speciality at Christmas time, made of marzipan dough shaped in forms to make little cookies, and decorated with half almonds.

**Frankfurter Kranz:** a special kind of cake that is baked in a form with a hole in the middle, sliced horizontally twice and filled with buttercream and often with red jam, then completely covered with buttercream and sprinkled with croquante and sliced almonds.

**Frankfurter Wurst:** thin boiled sausage made only from pork in casing that gets its

■ **Chez Ima**
Niddastrasse 58
Tel 069/256677280
▲ Hauptbahnhof
◆ 11.30-3pm, 6-11pm

In the restaurant of the design hotel 25hours you get home cooking the way mother does it – but the mothers come from different cultures. Cult status!

■ **Coq au Vin**
Textorstrasse 89 (Sachsenhausen)
Tel. 069/96200338
▲ Schweizer Platz, Frankfurt Süd
◆ from 5pm

Osteria Enoteca

From paté de foie gras, oysters and lobster to coq au vin, here you can enjoy the French way of living.

■ **Goldman Restaurant**
Hanauer Landstrasse 127 (Ostend)
Tel. 069/4058689806
▲ Ostbahnhof, Osthafenplatz
◆ Mon-Fri noon-3 pm, Mon-Sat 6pm-midnight

Design restaurant with a stylish interior that produces creative interpretations of classic German and Mediterranean dishes.

■ **Knoblauch**
Staufenstrasse 39 (Westend)
Tel. 069/722828
▲ Westend
◆ Mon-Fri 12 noon-2pm, 6.30pm-1am

A Frankfurt institution with exquisite cuisine française.

Osteria Enoteca

■ **La Cigale**
Falkstrasse 38 (Bockenheim)
Tel. 069/704111
▲ Leipziger Strasse
◆ from 6 pm

A small restaurant where the menu revolves around specialities of French and Mediterranean cuisine.

■ **Opera**
Opernplatz 1 (city centre)
Tel. 069/1340215
▲ Alte Oper
◆ noon-3 pm, from 6 pm

For a business lunch, Saturday treat, gourmet menu or Sunday brunch, the exceptional ambience of the historic foyer of the Alte Oper is always worth a visit.

Goldmann 25Hours Restaurant

## ■ Oosten – Realwirtschaft am Main
Mayfarthstrasse 4 (Ostend)
▲ Ostbahnhof
◆ Mon-Thu 10am-midnight, Fri 10am-1am, Sat 9am-1am, Sun 9am-10.30pm

With its all-round windows, this restaurant near the European Central Bank provides a view of the Frankfurt skyline to go with soul food and more.

## ■ Orfeo's Erben
Hamburger Allee 45 (Bockenheim)
Tel. 069/70769100
▲ Varrentrappstrasse
◆ Mon-Fri 11.30am-3pm, 6pm-11pm, Sat 6pm-11pm

Unconventional and popular cinema-restaurant with delicious food.

## ■ Sushimoto
Konrad-Adenauer-Strasse 7/ Arabella-Passage
Entrance on Grosse Friedberger Strasse/The Westin Grand, Frankfurt (city centre)
Tel. 069/1310057
▲ Konstablerwache
◆ Tue-Sat noon-2.30pm Tue-Sun 6pm-9.30pm

The best place in Frankfurt to eat Japanese!

## ■ Surf 'n Turf
Grüneburgweg 95 (Westend)
Tel. 069/722122
▲ Simon-Bolivar-Anlage, Grüneburgweg
◆ Mon-Fri noon-3pm, Mon-Sat 6pm-midnight

Here you can enjoy the national dish of American brokers – steak and lobster on one plate – cooked to an extremely high standard.

## ■ Zarges Gourmet Restaurant
Kalbächer Gasse 10 (city centre)
Tel. 069/299030
▲ Hauptwache
◆ Mon-Sat 11 am-midnight

Gourmet restaurant where one of Germany's best chefs cooks the very finest French and Mediterranean cuisine.

*Frankfurt specialities*

distinctive taste from a special method of smoking.

**Grüne Sauce:** a cold herb sauce served with meat, fish or potatoes, traditionally prepared from seven herbs: borage, chervil, cress, parsley, pimpernel, sorrel and chives.

**Haddekuchen:** diamond-shaped spicy biscuit covered with a diamond pattern.

**Handkäs mit Musik:** mature cheese made from sour milk that has been marinaded in chopped onions, vinegar, oil, caraway seeds, salt and pepper. To eat it you don't use a fork, but cut off a slice with your knife, place it on the bread or the point of the knife and transfer to the mouth.

**Kreppel:** a kind of doughnut made of sweet yeast dough fried in fat and filled with jam.

**Rippche:** a chop that has been mildly salted by marinading, eaten with sauerkraut or mustard and a slice of rustic bread.

# Pubs and Beer Gardens

*A glass of a good vintage in the wine cellar, apple wine in a traditional tavern or beer in a pub: there is a wide choice of places to spend an evening in Frankfurt.*

**Old Sachsenhausen**
As an entertainment quarter Dribbdebach, which means "over there across the Main" and refers to the district around Grosse Rittergasse, is known far beyond the Frankfurt city limits. Narrow cobbled lanes and timber-framed buildings set the scene here in the apple-wine ("Ebbelwoi") quarter, which is a hotspot for nightlife thanks to the atmospheric Ebbelwoi taverns. Sachsenhausen takes its name from the Saxons, who are said to have been settled here by Charlemagne after he defeated them.

■ **Bockenheimer Weinkontor**
Schlossstrasse 92/Hinterhaus (Bockenheim)
▲ Varrentrappstrasse
◆ from 6pm

The garden in summer and the warm fireplace in winter make this former smithy a popular spot to meet for a glass of wine and a tasty snack.

■ **Fichtekränzi**
Wallgasse 5 (Sachsenhausen)
▲ Affentorplatz
◆ from 5pm, Sun from 4pm

One of Frankfurt's oldest apple-wine taverns has introduced some new ideas: friendly waiters, varied and not just regional food, wines by the glass, draught beer and eau de vie from Alsace.

■ **Frankfurter Küche**
Hanauer Landstrasse 86 (Ostend)
▲ Ostbahnhof
◆ Mon-Fri 11am-3pm, Mon-Sat 5pm-midnight

Trendy corner pub where Handkäs mit Musik and other delicacies are on the menu. DJ programme late in the evening.

■ **Gerbermühle**
Gerbermühlstrasse 105
▲ Deutschherrnufer
◆ Summer garden from 11.30am, restaurant 11.30 am-10pm

Day trippers and sunlovers flock to this summer garden on the banks of the Main, as Goethe once did. Even when the weather is not warm, the restaurant in the conservatory serves excellent food.

Frankfurt Küche

■ **Jazzkeller Frankfurt**
Kleine Bockenheimer Strasse 18a (city centre)
▲ Alte Oper
Programme at *www.jazzkeller.com*

A world-famous Frankfurt institution: go down the steps to Germany's oldest jazz club, an intimate venue with international stars since 1952.

■ **Leon Garcias**
Walther-von-Cronberg-Platz 1 (Sachsenhausen)
▲ Lokalbahnhof
◆ from noon

Treat yourself to tapas and other especialidadas on the lovely terrace.

■ **Mampf**
Sandweg 64 (Ostend)
▲ Merianplatz
◆ Mon-Thu 6pm-1am, Fri-Sat 6pm-2am

Jazz, blues and other styles have featured on the programme here for over 35 years.

■ **Solzer-Apfelwein-wirtschaft**
Berger Strasse 260 (Bornheim)
▲ Bornheim-Mitte, Saalburger Strasse
◆ 12.30 am-10 pm

An apple-wine tavern in Bornheim with an atmospheric courtyard, old-established and always crowded.

■ **Zum gemalten Haus**
Schweizer Strasse 67 (Sachsenhausen)
▲ Schweizer Platz, Schwanthalerstrasse
◆ Tue-Sun 10am-midnight

An authentic Frankfurt apple-wine pub with cult status, lots of wall paintings and down-to-earth regional cooking.

■ **Zur Stalburg**
Glauburgstrasse 80 (Nordend)
▲ Glauburgstrasse
◆ from 5pm

Genuine apple-wine pub with a beer garden and a theatre next door. Here you can enjoy solid Hessian food and drink delicious apple wine by the jug.

■ **Vinum**
Kleine Hochstrasse 9 (city centre)
▲ Alte Oper
◆ Mon-Fri 4pm-1am, Sat 5pm-1am

An attractive wine cellar, popular after opera performances and worth a stop any time.

**Ebbelwei-Eppelwoi-Äppelwei-Äppelwoi**
In High German the national drink of the Frankfurt area is called "Apfelwein", but the locals have their own

ways of pronouncing and spelling it. Ebbelwoi, fermented apple juice, has a long tradition in this region. It is made by pressing local apples and can be drunk at various stages: Süsser is freshly pressed after harvesting, Rauscher has fermented for just a few weeks, Neuer has been fully fermented. Whether drunk straight or as a Gespritzter (diluted with mineral water), it is always served in an earthenware jug known as a Bembel and drunk from a Gerippter, a glass with a ribbed surface.

# Bars & Nightlife

*For a pre-dinner cocktail, a drink after the opera or to dance the night away, with a view of the skyline or in the dim light of a cellar – Frankfurt's nightlife has it all!*

## Frankfurt's Vital Statistics

With a population of nearly 700,000, Frankfurt is the largest city in Hesse and the fifth-largest in Germany. About a quarter of the residents are foreign nationals. Around 25 per cent are Roman Catholic, 22 per cent Protestant and 11 per cent Muslim.

The city boundary has a length of 113 kilometres. The greatest extent of the city territory is 23.4 kilometres from east to west and 23.3 kilometres from north to south. Out of a surface area of more than 250 square kilometres, 32 per cent is built-up or unoccupied, 17.8 per cent is used for traffic and 15 per cent is woodland. The highest point lies at 212 metres, the lowest at 88 metres above sea level.

■ **22nd Lounge**
Neue Mainzer Strasse 66–68 (in the Eurotheum/ city centre)
▲ Willy-Brandt-Platz
◆ Mon-Sat 6pm-1am

Sip your cocktail on the 22nd floor of the Innside Frankfurt Eurotheum with a glittering view of Frankfurt.

■ **Bar im Bristol Hotel Frankfurt**
Ludwigstrasse 15 (near main station)
▲ Festhalle/Messe, Platz der Republik
◆ 8-2am

For a business meeting, to kick off a night on the town or a nightcap, this trendy bar near the railway station is open round the clock.

■ **Chinanski**
Bockenheimer Landstr. 1-3 (city centre)
▲ Taunusanlage, Alte Oper
◆ Tue-Mon 8pm-2am, Thu-Sat 8pm-4am

A cross between a bar and a club, with graffiti on bare walls. Come here for a chat over a cocktail or to dance all night.

■ **Club Travolta**
Brönnerstraße 17 (city centre)
▲ Konstablerwache
◆ Tue, Thu-Sat from 11pm

If you get night fever, dance your way back to the 1970s. The programme also includes hip hop and R'n'B-Classics: www.club-travolta.de.

■ **Cooky's**
Am Salzhaus 4 (city centre)
▲ Hauptwache
◆ Tue–Sat from 11pm

The club's motto is "best sound in town", and it has everything party-goers are looking for.

■ **Gekkos**
(in the Hilton)
Hochstrasse 4 (city centre)
▲ Eschenheimer Tor
◆ From 6pm

An elegant hotel bar with prize-winning cocktails and more than 80 kinds of whisky, which you can accompany with exquisite cigars.

■ **Gibson Club**
Zeil 85-93 (city centre)
▲ Konstablerwache
*www.gibson-club.de*

Jimmy's Bar

Long Island Summer Lounge

One of the trendiest clubs in Frankfurt, with concerts on weekdays and well-known DJs at weekends.

■ **Jimmy's Bar**
Friedrich-Ebert-Anlage 40 (trade fair, in the Hotel Hessischer Hof)
▲ Messe
◆ 8pm-4am

The classic Frankfurt bar: an American bar with pleasant piano music and good cocktails.

■ **Long Island Summer Lounge**
Parkhaus Börse, park level 7 (6th floor)
Entrance on Meisengasse or Kaiserhofstrasse 12 (city centre)
▲ Alte Oper
◆ Mon-Sat 4pm-1am
Sun 2pm-1am

A wonderful sun deck high above the roofs of Frankfurt, where you can gaze on the skyline of Mainhattan while enjoying club sounds and cocktails.

■ **Main Tower**
Neue Mainzer Strasse 52–58 (city centre)
▲ Taunusanlage
◆ Tue-Thu 6pm-midnight, Fri-Sat 6pm-1am

The 53rd floor of Frankfurt's first skyscraper that is open to the public is the place to be for cocktails and also recommended for fine dining.

■ **The Parlour**
Zwingergasse 6 (city centre)
▲ Hauptwache
◆ Mon-Wed 8pm-2am, Thu-Sat 8pm-3am

The Parlour is hidden away. Here you can drink excellent cocktails while seated on dark brown Chesterfield sofas. To gain admission, knock on the dark glass.

■ **The Place to Be**
Weissadlergasse 3 (city centre)
▲ Hauptwache
◆ Mon-Sat noon-1 am

Small bar with atmosphere and outstanding cocktails.

### *Frankfurt's Vital Statistics*

The city lies on both sides of the river Main in the south-east of the Taunus region and is divided into 46 districts. Frankfurt is famous for its skyline, which includes some of Europe's tallest skyscrapers. The highest building is the Commerzbank Tower at 259 metres, followed by the Messeturm at 257 metres.

A large number of branches of national and international companies, the seat of the European Central Bank and the Frankfurt stock exchange make the city one of Europe's leading business centres. With the airport, main railway station and the Frankfurter Kreuz autobahn intersection, Frankfurt is also one of Europe's most important transport hubs.

# Wellness + Health

*For beauty treatments, floating massage and much more, Frankfurt boasts many spas where you can recuperate from everyday stress and let your soul relax.*

**Chinese Garden**
A wooden gate guarded by two lions leads into this garden, which was laid out by Chinese craftsmen on an area of 4000 square metres according to the classical principles of feng shui and the lore of harmony. A little pond, a marble bridge, various pavilions and a stepped gateway adorned with dragons make it a place to linger and meditate. The Chinese Garden is at the heart of the Bethmannpark, which originated as the "garden at the city gates" owned by the banking family of the same name. Today, surrounded by thick walls, it is a leafy oasis amid the bustle of the city.

◆ Mon-Fri from 7am, Sat-Sun from 10am, until dusk

■ **Emotion Spa im Westin Grand Hotel**
Konrad-Adenauer-Str. 7 (city centre)
Tel. 069/29819792
▲ Konstablerwache
◆ Mon-Fri 7am-10pm, Sat-Sun 8am-8pm
*www.emotionspa.de*

For hotel guests and everyone else too: a comprehensively equipped gym, aqua-fitness training and a sauna for relaxation afterwards.

■ **Heaven Spa im Radisson BLU Hotel**
Franklinstrasse 65 (Bockenheim)
Tel. 069/7701550
▲ Westbahnhof, An der Dammweide
◆ Mon-Fri 10am-10pm, Sat-Sun 10am-8pm
*www.radissonblu.de/hotel-frankfurt*

This health club with a breathtaking view of the Frankfurt skyline tempts its guests to linger with a pool, sauna, steam bath, solarium, gym area and massage.

■ **Lilu**
Niederräder Ufer 10 (Sachsenhausen)
▲ Heinrich-Hoffmann-Strasse/Blutspendedienst
◆ From 11am until dusk
*www.lilu-frankfurt.de*

A public beach and river bathing area on the Main with a snack island from the Biennale.

■ **Lindner Hotel & Residence Main Plaza**
Beauty & Spa
Walther-von-Cronberg-Platz 1 (Sachsenhausen)
Tel. 069/664013203
▲ Lokalbahnhof
◆ Mon-Fri 12.30pm-9pm, Sat-Sun 10am-6pm
*www.lindner.de*

Switch off, take a deep breath, relax and be pampered in the hotel's beauty parlour and spa with a swimming pool, saunas, steam bath and the latest gym apparatus.

■ **Panoramabad**
Inheidener Strasse 60 (Bornheim)
Tel. 069/2710891300
▲ Panoramabad
◆ Wed-Mon 8am-10pm, Thu women's sauna
*www.bbf-frankfurt.de*

The attractions here are the panorama jacuzzi and the

Titus Thermen

Hilton Frankfurt Hotel

sauna landscape with an outdoor log cabin.

**■ Rebstockbad**
Zum Rebstockbad 7 (Bockenheim)
Tel. 069/708078
▲ Rebstockbad
◆ Mon 2pm-10pm, Tue-Sun 10am-10pm, Tue + Thu women's sauna
*www.bbf-frankfurt.de*

Frankfurt's top water paradise has an extensive Japanese-style sauna area, a wave pool and sports pools that provide fun and relaxation for all.

**■ Rhein Main Therme**
Niederhofheimer Strasse 67
65719 Hofheim
Tel. 06192/977790
▲ Hofheim am Taunus + In den Nassen/Therme
◆ 9am-11pm
*www.rhein-main-therme.de*

An 18,000-square-metre area devoted to fun and fitness to make you feel good and forget the cares of the world with pools, saunas and gym.

**■ River Wellness**
Zum Apothekerhofe (Sachsenhausen)
Tel. 069/66377745
▲ Hauptwache
◆ Wed-Mon noon-8pm
*www.riverwellness.de*

Massage, physiotherapy and beauty treatments - whatever you desire.

**■ The Spa im Steigenberger Frankfurter Hof**
Am Kaiserplatz (Bahnhofsviertel)
▲ Hauptbahnhof
◆ 10am-10pm
*www.thespa.steigenberger.com*

This luxurious spa offers beauty treatments, relaxation rituals and spa treatments from all over the world.

**■ Titus Thermen**
Walter-Möller-Platz 2 (Niederursel)
Tel. 069/2710891200
▲ Nordwestzentrum
◆ 10am-10pm, Mon + Wed women's sauna
*www.titusthermen-frankfurt.de*

Roman-style baths and a sauna area of over 2000 square metres with light and sound effects for pure relaxation.

**■ Villa Kennedy**
Kennedyallee 70 (Sachsenhausen)
Tel. 069/717121160
▲ Stresemannallee/Gartenstrasse
◆ 6.30am-10pm
*www.villakennedyhotel.de*

A world away from stress and bustle, this five-star spa offers a comprehensive range of treatments for residents and day guests.

**Korean Garden**
South Korea was guest country at the Frankfurt Book Fair in 2005, and made a special gift to the city: a 4800-square-metre garden in the middle of the Grüneburgpark in the style of a traditional scholar's garden, laid out according to the principle of the seasons, with two pavilions, two ponds and plants such as the pine, bamboo and plum tree as symbols of long life. Just as such gardens served as a retreat for Korean artists and intellectuals from the 16th century, the Korean Garden is intended as a place of peace and leisure for the people of Frankfurt.

◆ from 8am until dusk

# Culture

*Frankfurt's cultural scene has everything – not just Goethe and the Museumsmeile, but classical music, jazz and dance, theatre, variety shows, cabaret and literature.*

## Music & Dance

**■ Alte Oper**
Opernplatz (city centre)
Tel. 069/134000
▲ Alte Oper
*www.alteoper.de*

Under the direction of Stephan Pauly, the programme of high-calibre performers every evening offers great diversity, from early Baroque to avant-garde music, from family concerts and musicals to jazz, rock and pop.

**■ Dresden Frankfurt Dance Company**
Bockenheimer Depot
Schmidtstrasse 12
(Bockenheim)
Tel. 069/907399100
▲ Bockenheimer Warte
*www.dresdenfrankfurt-dancecompany.com*

When not on tour, choreographer William Forsythe's renowned company performs contemporary dance in the Bockenheimer Depot.

Hr-Bigband

**■ Oper Frankfurt**
Willy-Brandt-Platz
(city centre)
Tel. 069/21249494
▲ Willy-Brandt-Platz
*www.oper-frankfurt.de*

This programme at this long-established opera house, one of the best in Europe under the direction of Bernd Loebe, includes works by Mozart, Strauss, Verdi and Wagner, rarely-performed and contemporary operas, Lieder evenings and chamber music.

**■ Papageno-Musiktheater im Palmengarten**
Siesmayerstrasse (Westend)
Tel. 069/1340400
▲ Bockenheimer Warte
*www.papageno-theater.de*

Under its dome amidst the greenery of the Palmengarten this ensemble stages musical theatre and pieces based on the great operas for young and old.

**■ Hr-Bigband**
Bertramstrasse 8 (Nordend)
Tel. 069/1552000
*www.hr-online.de*

One more pillar of the city's reputation as a cultural centre: the old dance orchestra of Radio Frankfurt has become a renowned jazz big-band with the confidence to cross the borders between classical music and pop, between exotic and electronic music.

**Jazzgass ...**
... (jazz alley) is Kleine Bockenheimer Strasse, the site of Frankfurt's most famous jazz venue since 1952: the Jazzkeller. Founded by a musician, Carlo Bohländer, it quickly became an institution for both performers and audiences. Jazz greats such as Ella Fitzgerald, Duke Ellington and Chet Baker have played here. Frankfurt also owes its reputation as a jazz city to the world's oldest jazz festival, initiated in 1953 by the concert organiser of the German Jazz Federation, Horst Lippmann, and run since 1984 by the regional broadcaster, Hessischer Rundfunk. To this day the Deutsches Jazzfestival promotes new talent, brings about remarkable encounters between musicians and combines the skills of artists across genres.

*www.jazzfestival.hr-online.de*

Oper Frankfurt/Barbara Aumüller

■ **Kammeroper Frankfurt**
Sternstrasse 31
Tel. 069/556189
*www.kammeroper-frankfurt.de*

This independent opera ensemble, which describes itself as "a shifting dune on the city's cultural scene", performs opera buffa, operetta, comic opera and modern operas in unusual locations such as an old brewery-pub.

English Theatre

■ **Junge Deutsche Philharmonie**
Schwedlerstrasse 2–4 (Ostend)
Tel. 069/94343050
*www.jdph.de*

This orchestra with Germany's most talented young musicians puts on concerts of the highest standard and provides a new experience of music.

## *Theatre*

■ **Ampere Theater**
Berger Strasse 316 (Bornheim)
Tel. 069/7384161
▲ Bornheim Mitte
*www.ampere-theater.de*

Improvised theatre that brings down the house: if the audience so desires, the ensemble is capable of changing the programme from a musical to a horror show.

■ **Die Käs**
Waldschmidtstrasse 19 (Bornheim)
Tel. 069/550736
▲ Merianplatz, Zoo
*www.diekaes.de*

This must be the only Turkish satire that is staged in German: Sinasi Dikmen's political and literary barbs are known nationwide. Käs is an abbreviation of "tailor's cabaret", but also means "cheese".

■ **Die Komödie**
Neue Mainzer Strasse 14–18 (city centre)
Tel. 069/284580
▲ Willy-Brandt-Platz
*www.diekomoedie.de*

Good-quality humorous entertainment has been performed on this stage since 1950.

■ **Freies Schauspiel**
Basaltstrasse 23 (Bockenheim)
▲ Leipziger Strasse
Tel. 069/71913020
*www.freiesschauspiel.de*

For over 20 years the ensemble has put its stamp on this theatre, earning enthusiastic responses from critics and audiences.

**Dresden Frankfurt Dance Company**
There is probably no single person who has had a more radical influence on attitudes to dance than the choreographer William Forsythe. Regarded as one of the foremost representatives of contemporary dance, he has redefined classical ballet and made it into a new, dynamic art form for the 21st century. His choreographic thought has evolved continuously through contact to the pioneering international movements in contemporary art, and at the same time has contributed to them: from performance art and the fine arts to architecture and interactive multimedia work. Since 2015 Jacopo Godani, once a dancer in Forsythe´s ballet company, has continued this tradition under a new name: Dresden Frankfurt Dance Company.

*www.dresdenfrankfurt-dancecompany.com*

# Culture

**Mousonturm Arts Centre**
Where soap and perfume were produced until the 1970s, today one of the internationally most important and successful free centres of art production is based. The Expressionist-style tower of the former Mouson soap factory, a protected monument with more than 4000 square metres of space, is a place for exchanges of ideas. It is used not only for theatre and contemporary dance projects, choreography and performance art, but also has a programme of contemporary music, visual arts, films, concerts and installations.

*www.mousonturm.de*

■ **Internationales Theater**
Hanauer Landstrasse 5–7
(Ostend)
Tel. 069/4930503
▲ Ostendstrasse
*www.internationales-theater.de*

Artists and ensembles from all over the world present the performing arts of their homeland, from drama to dance and concerts, in addition to exhibitions and readings.

■ **Die Schmiere**
Seckenbächer Gasse 4
(city centre)
Tel. 069/281066
▲ Willy-Brandt-Platz
*www.die-schmiere.de*

One of Germany's classic satirical cabaret groups stages its own unique mixture of political cabaret, variety show and comedy in the cellar of the Carmelite monastery.

■ **Neues Theater Höchst**
Emmerich-Josef-Straße 46a
(Höchst)
Tel. 069/3399990
▲ Höchster Bahnhof
*www.neues-theater.de*

A diverse mix of cabaret, music, cinema, and the house's own varieté programme.

■ **schauspielfrankfurt**
Neue Mainzer Straße 17
(city centre)
Tel. 069/21249494
▲ Willy-Brandt-Platz
*www.schauspielfrankfurt.de*

Aeschylus, Shakespeare and Sartre, classic authors and young dramatists, plays from ancient to modern times are performed at Frankfurt's city theatre under the direction of Elisabeth Schweeger.

■ **Stalburg Theater**
Glauburgstrasse 80
(Nordend)
Tel. 069/25627744
▲ Glauburgstrasse
*www.stalburg.de*

Every evening audiences are treated to chansons, jazz, cabaret or classical music in the ballroom of this old apple-wine tavern.

■ **The English Theatre Frankfurt**
Gallusanlage 7
(near main station)
Tel. 069/24231620
▲ Willy-Brandt-Platz
*www.english-theatre.de*

The English Theatre is one of the highlights of Frankfurt's cultural scene, and after enjoying some English-language

Papageno Musiktheater im Palmengarten

Oper Frankfurt/Barbara Aumüller

entertainment you can drink whisky at the theatre bar.

■ **Tigerpalast – Internationales Varieté Theater**
Heiligkreuzgasse 16–20
Tel. 069/9200220
▲ Konstablerwache
*www.tigerpalast.de*

The world's best artistes present top-class varieté and circus-style artistry in a breathtaking show each evening.

Freies Schauspiel

## Cinemas

■ **Berger Kino**
Berger Strasse 177 (Bornheim)
Tel. 069/ 9450330
▲ Bornheim Mitte
*www.berger-kino-frankfurt-am-main.kino-zeit.de*

Arthouse cinema with lots of atmosphere but also the latest digital projection technology.

■ **Cinestar Metropolis**
Eschenheimer Anlage 40 (city centre)
Tel. 069/ 95506401
▲ Eschenheimer Tor
*www.cinestar.de*

Multiplex with a programme of commercial cinema in the usual quality.

■ **Filmforum Höchst**
Emmerich-Josef-Strasse 46a (Höchst)
Tel. 069/21249494
▲ Höchst Bahnhof
*www.filmforum-hoechst.de*

If you like films that are definitely not mainstream, the special series and thematic programmes screened here are just the thing.

■ **Orfeo's Erben**
Hamburger Allee 45 (Bockenheim)
Tel. 069/70769100
▲ Naunheimer Strasse
*www.orfeos.de*

In this cinema-restaurant you can recline in first-class Lufthansa seats to enjoy arthouse films with fantastic sound quality.

## Literature

■ **Literaturhaus Frankfurt**
Schöne Aussicht 2 (city centre)
Tel. 069/7561840
▲ Hospital zum Heiligen Geist, Schöne Aussicht
*www.literaturhaus-frankfurt.de*

The place for readings, literary discussions and other events connected with literature.

**Book fair**
"Here is the fair, quick, unpack and decorate your stand, come, authors, all of you, and try your luck," wrote Goethe about the event that is now the world's largest and most important specialist fair for publishers, authors, journalists and others, and has a history going back to the early days of printing. Organised since 1949 by the Börsenverein des Deutschen Buchhandels, it has over 7000 exhibitors from 100 countries and almost 275,000 visitors every year. At each fair the book production and culture of a guest country are presented. The highlights are the award of the Peace Prize of the German Book Trade and the prize for German Youth Literature.

*www.buchmesse.de*

# Museums

*A fine variety of museums and galleries have established Frankfurt's reputation as a city of art and culture. The spectrum of themes in the museums here takes in architecture, film, icons and transport.*

**Struwwelpeter**
Generations of children have read about Struwwelpeter, the eponymous character in a book that has been translated into 35 languages. Although not uncontroversial, it is still one of the best-known children's books. In 1844 Heinrich Hoffmann, a Frankfurt doctor, finding nothing suitable for his three-year-old son, drew stories of children who are not well-behaved, don't listen to their parents and therefore have to suffer unpleasant happenings. A museum in a beautifully restored villa in the Westend illuminates the influence of the book and the personality of the author, and looks at other children's books.

Schubertstrasse 20 (Westend)
▲ Westend
◆ Tue-Sun 10am-5pm
*www.struwwelpeter-museum.de*

**■ Archäologisches Museum**
Karmelitergasse 1 (city centre)
▲ Willy-Brandt-Platz
◆ Tue, Thu-Sun 10am-6pm, Wed 10am-8pm
*www.archaeologisches-museum.frankfurt.de*

In the reconstructed Carmelite church you can find out all about the early history of the settlement on the river Main.

**■ Deutsches Architekturmuseum**
Schaumainkai 43 (Museumsufer)
▲ Schweizer Platz
◆ Tue, Thu-Sun 11am - 6pm, Wed 11am-8pm
*www.dam-online.de*

The museum is devoted to milestones in architecture.

**■ Deutsches Filmmuseum**
➤ p. 23

**■ Dialogmuseum**
Hanauer Landstrasse 137–145 (Ostend)
▲ Osthafenplatz
◆ Tue-Fri 9am-5pm, Sat-Sun 11am-7pm
*www.dialogmuseum.de*

A museum for exploring the senses: blind guides take visitors through an exhibition entitled "Dialogue in the Dark".

**■ Dommuseum**
➤ p. 19

**■ Frankfurter Kunstverein**
➤ p. 18

**■ Goethe-Museum**
➤ p. 14

**■ Historisches Museum**
Fahrtor 2 (city centre)
▲ Dom/Römer
◆ Tue-Sun 10am-6pm, Wed 10am-9pm
*www.historisches-museum.frankfurt.de*

The history of Frankfurt from the early Middle Ages to the present day.

**■ Ikonenmuseum**
Brückenstrasse 3–7 (Sachsenhausen)
▲ Elisabethenstrasse
◆ Tue, Thu-Sun 10am-5pm, Wed 10am-8pm
*www.ikonenmuseum frankfurt.de*

Here you can find out about the importance of icons for worship.

**■ Jüdisches Museum**
Untermainkai 14/15 (city centre)
▲ Willy-Brandt-Platz
◆ Tue 10am-8pm, Wed-Sun 10am-6pm
*www.juedischesmuseum.de*

Historisches Museum

The exhibitions in the former Rothschild Palais are devoted to the history of Jewish life in Frankfurt.

■ **Liebieghaus - Museum alter Plastik**
➤ p. 24

■ **Museum für Angewandte Kunst**
Schaumainkai 17 (Museumsufer)
▲ Schweizer Platz
◆ Tue, Thu-Sun 10am-6pm, Wed 10am-8pm
*www.museumangewandtekunst.de*

Digital crafts and product design are presented in addition to departments for European, Islamic and Far Eastern arts and crafts.

■ **Museum für Komische Kunst (Caricatura-Museum)**
Weckmarkt 17
◆ Tue, Thu-Sun 11am-6pm, Wed 11am-9pm
*www.caricatura-museum.de*

In the historic Leinwandhaus more than 4,000 original cartoons from the legendary Frankfurt School can be viewed.

■ **Museum für Kommunikation**
Schaumainkai 53 (Museumsufer)
▲ Schweizer Platz
◆ Tue-Fri 9am-6pm, Sat-Sun 11am-7pm
*www.mfk-frankfurt.de*

The exhibition here is all about communications.

■ **Museum für Moderne Kunst**
➤ p. 13

■ **Museum der Weltkulturen und Galerie 37**
Schaumainkai 29–37 (Sachsenhausen)
▲ Schweizer Platz
◆ Tue, Thu-Sun 11am-6pm, Wed 11am-8pm
*www.weltkulturenmuseum.de*

What used to be called the Museum für Völkerkunde organises exhibitions on global themes, and the gallery shows contemporary art from America, Africa, Oceania and Indonesia.

■ **Museum Giersch**
Schaumainkai 83 (Sachsenhausen)
▲ Stresemannallee/ Gartenstrasse
◆ Tue-Thu noon-7pm, Fri-Sun 10am-6pm
*www.museum-giersch.de*

In Villa Holzmann frequent temporary exhibitions are held on the theme of the "Rhein-Main cultural landscape".

■ **Museum Judengasse**
➤ p. 13

■ **Naturmuseum Senckenberg**
➤ p. 33

■ **Schirn-Kunsthalle**
➤ p. 18

■ **Städel**
➤ p. 36

**Money Museum**
You always have to pay, whether the currency is shells, cocoa beans or coins. In the Geldmuseum der Deutschen Bundesbank (federal bank) you can find out what means of payment have been used since ancient times and how to tell genuine from counterfeit money. This interesting exhibition covers all aspects of money, explaining even complex subjects such as how money works, inflation and deflation, monetary policy and the central bank. And if you feel inclined to buy a briquette made from a million in shredded euro notes, then go to the museum shop.

Wilhelm-Epstein-Strasse 14 (Ginnheim)
▲ Dornbusch
◆ Mon-Tue, Thu-Fri, Sun 10am-5pm, Wed 10am-8pm
*www.geldmuseum.de*

# Shopping

*Whatever you are looking for – something sweet as a gift, unusual design objects, exclusive fashion or hifi – Frankfurt's shopping zones are an Eldorado.*

**Bethmännchen**
At Christmas time they are available everywhere: little balls, baked from egg white, ground almonds, icing sugar and rose water, decorated with three half almonds and glazed with egg yolk. These delicacies take their name from the banking family Bethmann, whose French chef, Jean Jacques Gautenier, is traditionally said to have invented them.

As the Bethmann family had four sons, the little cakes were originally decorated with four half almonds, but after the death of one of the sons, Heinrich, the fourth was left off.

### ■ Buch und Wein
Bergerstrasse 122 (Bornheim)
▲ Höhenstrasse
◆ Mon-Sat 10 am 8 pm

Literature to accompany the (mainly Spanish) wines: they sell cookbooks, wine books, novels, and crime stories in which wine is drunk.

### ■ Design Classics
Fahrgasse 1 (city centre)
▲ Dom/Römer
◆ Tue-Fri 3pm-6.30pm, Sat noon-4pm

Strange and well-known classic design from the Fifties to the Eighties.

### ■ Gate 05
Berger Strasse 46 (Bornheim)
▲ Merianplatz
◆ Mon-Fri 10am-7pm, Sat 10am-4pm

Products for everyone who likes to travel, this shop sells everything from eyeshades to sponge bags.

### ■ Höchster Porzellan Manufaktur Direktverkauf
Palleskestrasse 32 (Höchst)
▲ Bahnhof Höchst
◆ Mon-Fri 9.30am-6pm, Sat 9.30am-2pm

Höchst porcelain, decorated with the "wheel of Mainz", has been among Europe's finest for over 260 years. This is the factory outlet.

### ■ Itaba
Töngesgasse 42 (city centre)
▲ Hauptwache
◆ Mon-Fri 10.30am-6pm, Sat 10am-6pm

Lovers of Japanese tableware and furnishings have a wide choice here.

### ■ Jamin
Schweizer Strasse 54A (Sachsenhausen)
▲ Schweizer Platz
◆ Mon-Fri 10am-6pm, Sat 9.30am-3pm

More than 60 different kinds of home-made pralines and truffles, of which the highlight is the Römer, filled with apple schnapps.

### ■ Kulturothek
An der Kleinmarkthalle 7-9 (city centre)
▲ Hauptwache
◆ Mon-Fri 10am-6pm, Sat 10am-3pm

Whether slippers of Hesse or a Bembel dish towel, here you can find fancy souvenirs of Frankfurt.

■ **Lorey**
Schillerstrasse 16 (city centre)
▲ Hauptwache
◆ Mon-Sat 10am-7pm

For Alessi, Meissen or Rösle: this shop for household goods established over 200 years ago has everything for the kitchen, the table and fine living.

■ **Whisky Spirits**
Wallstrasse 23 (Sachsenhausen)
▲ Lokalbahnhof
◆ Tue-Fri 4pm-8pm, Sat 11am-5pm

A specialist shop for whisky fans that stocks a great range of single malts.

TeeDeUm

■ **Öldorado**
Mörfelder Landstrasse 109a (Sachsenhausen)
▲ Südbahnhof
◆ Tue-Fri noon-6pm, Sat 11am-3pm

Lovers of olive oil come here to find a wide selection of oils and all sorts of accessories.

■ **TeeDeUm**
Schweizer Strasse 54a (Sachsenhausen)
▲ Schweizer Platz
◆ Mon-Sat 10am-6.30pm

A sensual paradise with culinary delights such as tea and coffee, oil and vinegar, jam and honey. Most of the goods are supplied by small artisan producers.

■ **Töpferei Maurer**
Wallstrasse 5 (Sachsenhausen)
▲ Lokalbahnhof
◆ Mon-Fri 9 am - 6 pm, Sat 9 am-1 pm

For the typical Franfurt souvenir: a Bembel (apple-wine jug) – painted, decorated, with or without a slogan.

■ **Wohnen & Spielen**
Grosse Friedberger Strasse 32 (city centre)
▲ Konstablerwache
◆ Mon-Fri 10am-7pm, Sat 10am-5pm

For children's books, wooden toys, dolls or more, this shop is heaven for large and small children.

**Watering holes**
A little kiosk that sells drinks is known as a Trinkhalle in Frankfurt. This institution has a long tradition as a place for selling water. In the second half of the 19th century Trinkhallen sprang up everywhere to sell the new popular drink, sparkling mineral water. All over the city the Trinkhallen became meeting points, extending their product range to include alcoholic drinks, tobacco, fruit and sweets. To this day, almost every Frankfurter has his or her favourite Trinkhalle, which sells everything that people need when other shops have closed for the evening.

# Addresses

**Eintracht Frankfurt**
Football has been played here since 1899, which makes Eintracht Frankfurt one of the grand old clubs of German football. In 1959 the red-and-blacks won the German championship, a year later became the first German team to reach the final of the European Cup, and in 1963 were founder members of the Bundesliga. The team has won the German cup four times (in 1974, 1975, 1981 and 1988) and the UEFA Cup once, in 1980. After difficult times, Eintracht Frankfurt again play in the first Bundesliga division. Their stadium, the Commerzbank-Arena, was completely rebuilt in 2005 and with a capacity of more than 50,000 is one of Germany's ten largest.
*www.eintracht.de*

■ **Information**
Tourismus + Congress GmbH
Kaiserstrasse 56
Tel. 069/21238800
Fax 069/21237880
*www.frankfurt-tourismus.de*
*info@infofrankfurt.de*

■ **Tourist Information Hauptbahnhof (main station)**
at the main entrance
◆ Mon-Fri 8am-9pm, Sat-Sun 9am-6pm

■ **Tourist Information Römer**
Römerberg 27
◆ Mon-Fri 9.30am-5.30pm, Sat-Sun 10am-4pm

■ **Banks**
◆ The banks in Frankfurt have the customary opening hours (usually 9am-4pm).

■ **Deutsche Bahn (railway)**
Tel. 0180/5996633
*www.bahn.de*

■ **Airport**
Tel. 01805/3724636
*www.airportcity-frankfurt.de*

■ **Frankfurt-Card**
Tourists and citizens of Frankfurt who want to discover their own city can buy the Frankfurt Card for either one or two days. It provides free journeys on public local transport within the city limits including the airport, discounts on sightseeing tours, reduced admission to museums, the Oper Frankfurt, Schauspiel Frankfurt and other sights, as well as lower prices at selected restaurants, cafés, bars and some retail outlets. The Frankfurt Card is available from the tourist information office, at the airport, at the Hauptwache and the Ticketcorners, and in some hotels.

■ **Ticket sales**

**Frankfurt Ticket RheinMain GmbH**
Ticket sale place
B-Ebene Hauptwache
Tel. 069/1340400
*www.frankfurtticket.de*

**Best Tickets GmbH**
in der Zeilgalerie
c/o 4. Etage
Zeil 112-114 (city)
Tel. 069/20228
*www.journal-ticketshop.de*

■ **Media**

**Print:** Frankfurter Allgemeine Zeitung, Frankfurter Rundschau, Frankfurter Neue Presse, Journal Frankfurt

**TV and radio:** Hit Radio FFH, Frankfurt Radio, Main FM, Hessischer Rundfunk, Radio X

## ■ Hire cars

**Avis** 01805/217702
**Europcar** 01805/8000
**Hertz** 01805/333535
**Sixt** 01805/252525

## ■ Emergency

**Police:** Tel. 110

**Fire:** Tel. 112

**Emergency doctor:**
Tel. 19292

**Emergency dentist:**
Tel. 069/59795360

**Emergency pharmacy:**
www.aponet.de

**ADAC breakdown service:**
Tel. 01802/222222

## ■ Public transport

**Verkehrsgesellschaft Frankfurt am Main (VGF)**
Service telephone
069/19449
*www.vgf-ffm.de*

**VGF Customer Centre**
Kurt-Schumacher-Strasse 10
◆ Mon-Fri 8am-5pm

## ■ City tours

**Bus round trip (2.5 hrs)**
from bus stop Paulskirche/Römer
*www.stadtrundfahrten-frankfurt.de*

**Kulturothek**
An der Kleinmarkthalle 7–9
Tel. 069/281010
*www.kulturothek-frankfurt.de*

**KulTours**
Wolf-Christian Setzepfandt
Mauerweg 18
Tel. 069/94318863
*www.kultours-frankfurt.de*

**Freundeskreis Liebenswertes Frankfurt**
Tel. 069/684765
*www.frankfurt-liebenswert.de*

**Frankfurter Personenschifffahrt (boats)**
Tel. 069/1338370
*www.primus-line.de*

## ■ Taxi

Tel. 069/230001
*www.taxi-frankfurt.de*

## ■ Websites

With pages in English:
*www.frankfurt.de*
*www.frankfurt-tourismus.de*
*www.frankfurt.inside-city.de*
*www.kultur-frankfurt.de*
In German only:
*www.rhein-main.net*
*www.frankfurtlive.com*
*www.frankfurt-tipp.de*

3 TIP

**A Hot Tip: Airport Tours**
If you want to peek behind the scenes at Frankfurt Airport, going on an airport tour is an absolute must. The portfolio includes a Basic Tour, Sunset Tour, Fire Department Tour and XXL Tour. You can get more information on

*www.airporttours.frankfurt-airport.com/en*

# Frankfurt's History

The hill on which the Dom stands has been continuously settled since the Bronze Age.

**83/84** The hill became a Roman military base after Emperor Domitian's victorious campaign against the Chatti.

**8th century** A Frankish royal palace occupies the hill.

**22nd February 794** First mention in documents of "Franconovurd".

**843** Ludwig the German chooses Frankfurt as the site of a royal palace.

**856** Lothar II is the first king to be elected in Frankfurt, which is the scene of imperial politics and royal elections for centuries to come.

**1152** Frederick I (Barbarossa) is elected king in Frankfurt.

**1240** Frankfurt is granted the privilege of holding an annual autumn fair on the Römerberg.

**1266** First mention of the Frankfurt city council. A small number of patrician families holds power.

**1330** Ludwig IV of Bavaria gives permission for holding a second trade fair, in spring. Frankfurt is now established as a city of trade fairs.

**1356** The Golden Bull confirms Frankfurt's status as the place where German kings are elected.

**1372** Frankfurt is made an independent imperial city with sovereignty on financial, judicial and administrative matters.

**1381** Frankfurt joins the league of Rhenish cities.

**1480** The first book fair takes place in the Römer.

**1548** Frankfurt becomes a mixed city of Roman Catholics and Protestants.

**1562** With the coronation of Maximilian as Holy Roman Emperor, Frankfurt takes over from Aachen as the place of coronation.

**1585** The setting of currency and exchange rates by the merchants of the trade fair inaugurates exchange trading.

| | |
|---|---|
| **28 August 1749** | Birth of Johann Wolfgang Goethe. |
| **1810–13** | Grand Duchy of Frankfurt. |
| **1815** | Following the Congress of Vienna, Frankfurt remains a free city within the German Confederation and is the seat of the Federal Diet. |
| **18 May 1848** | First meeting of the National Assembly in the Paulskirche. |
| **1866** | Prussia annexes the city. |
| **1891** | Workers in Bockenheim found the Deutscher Metallarbeiter Verband, predecessor of the leading trade union IG Metall. |
| **1914** | Foundation of Frankfurt University. |
| **1926** | Under Mayor Ludwig Landmann the airport at Rebstock is opened. |
| **1943–44** | The old quarter is completely destroyed by bombing raids. |
| **Until 1949** | Frankfurt is provisional federal capital until the founding of the Federal Republic. |
| **1949** | First issue of the Frankfurter Allgemeine Zeitung newspaper. |
| **1 August 1957** | The Deutsche Bundesbank starts business in Frankfurt. |
| **1984** | The opening of the Filmmuseum and the Deutsches Architekturmuseum is the start of the expansion of the Museumsufer. |
| **1997** | The Commerzbank Tower, Europe's tallest office building at 259 metres, is completed. |
| **1998** | Frankfurt becomes seat of the European Central Bank. |
| **2006** | Matches of the football world cup are held in the Commerzbank-Arena. |
| **2010** | The twin towers of Deutsche Bank are converted to green buildings. |
| **2011** | The new north-west runway of the Rhein-Main Airport went into operation. |
| **2018** | The DomRömer Quarter is opened. |

## Index



## Picture credits